Practical
Strategies
for
Middle School
Inclusion

Eileen M. Bowers

IEP

RESOURCES

Author: Eileen M. Bowers

Edited By: Tom Kinney

Graphic Design: Sherry Pribbenow

An Attainment Company Publication

RESOURCES

P.O. Box 930160 • Verona, Wisconsin 53593-0160 • U.S.A.

Phone: 800-327-4269 • Fax: 800.942.3865

www.AttainmentCompany.com

ISBN: 1-57861-498-8

Contents

Preface/Acknowledgements

Eileen Bowers

For as long as I can remember, I have wanted to be a teacher. As a young child growing up, I watched my father as he involved himself with various youth organizations. While he'd never received formal education in the traditional classroom sense, he was one of the most successful teachers I have ever seen. The impact that his influence had on young people's lives was something I wanted to experience in my own life. Looking back on it now, I can't recall the exact moment I came to this realization. It became a part of me and set me on the course I continue to follow.

I began my journey into education at the University of Dayton. As an undergraduate student, I gravitated toward a career in special education and obtained elementary education and special education certificates. My first job was as a seventh grade general education teacher in Cleveland.

Next, I had the opportunity to become a certified classroom assistant, which fit perfectly with my desire to begin a family. This was my introduction into special education in a public school setting.

It was the mid 70's, and House Bill 94-142 was being implemented. Many children with special needs were being afforded a free and appropriate public education for the first time. In reality however, this was not entirely true. Our public school system had begun offering special education programs, but these children were not included with the rest of the school population. They typically rode on separate buses, arrived later than the mainstream and left earlier, and were educated in segregated rooms. None of this was done by malicious intent. It was the beginning of a new era for education and decisions were made with everyone's best interest in mind. I have been fortunate to be in the field during interesting times. Upon the inception of 94-142, to think that children with special needs could be successfully educated alongside regular students would have been a difficult concept to grasp. We really have come a long way.

Teaching was a wonderful profession to be involved in while raising a family and much of what I learned I was able to apply at home in my roll as parent. My husband, John, and I have three wonderful boys, Brendan, Kevin and Trevor and when I am not teaching we spend much of our time together. We find great enjoyment in watching our boys in athletics: Brendan played basketball into his college days; Kevin ended his high school football career as captain of a state title team; and Trevor is a high school wrestler. In addition, Kevin is working toward a teaching license at the University of Dayton.

It is because of my family that I have been able to do the things I do. My husband has always been my greatest supporter. A few years ago when I told him I wanted to write a book, he didn't hesitate for a minute. Without his support and encouragement, I couldn't have gotten through it.

To date, I've had a rewarding career, and I've seen growth in the way we as educators relate with and teach children. This has been due in part to insightful administrators who I have worked with. They have been willing to "think outside the box" and design programs that were best for kids. The first I would like to mention is Mrs. Rolanda Schonauer.

When I came to her after my first inservice on inclusion in 1990, my colleague, Kerry Bowser and I shared what we had learned about implementing it in our building. Our suggestions were met with openness and a willingness to work on making it a success. Due to the newness of the idea, none of us knew how to implement it but we knew we wanted to make it work. Rolanda spent many hours observing people who were beginning to practice inclusion, and together we spent about a year gathering information through researching, dialoguing and observing. Fortunately, it's evolved into a way of life at Eastlake Middle School thanks in part to Mrs. Schonauer.

Mr. Buddy Young and Mrs. Jane Sweeney are the next two administrators I want to thank. He gave me the idea to write this book, and she was generous enough to share her vast knowledge on special education with me. She has worked in the field for years and was always willing to talk through ideas and to help in any way she could.

Anyone who has tried inclusion knows the hardest part is getting professionals together in an effective, cohesive fashion. I want to thank my cousin Bob Garrity for helping me in this area. His successful work as a mediator has given him insight and wisdom on human relationships that he was willing to share with me. He has written a section on working relationships we have included in this book (Chapter 9, pages 129-157).

I also want to thank my two colleagues, Kim Hugh and Karen Finnegan, who helped this program become successful. Special and regular education cannot come together unless the teachers are willing to come together for the good of all students. These two women are professionals in every aspect of the word. Our students have grown as a direct result of their generosity and openness to teach all types of children.

1

What Makes Inclusion Work?

Characteristics of a Successful Inclusion Program

IDEAS '97 and '02 have sent educators into a tailspin.
Up until this point, everyone's role was well understood.
Special education teachers were responsible for their
students and regular education teachers were responsible for
their students. On occasion, a high functioning special
education student was mainstreamed into the regular
education class, but not many accommodations were made
for that child. If he didn't "cut it" in the mainstream, he was
pulled. It was very simple and clearly defined. With the
introduction of IDEAs '97 and '02 and the push to have more
special education students included within the general
curriculum, responsibilities of teachers and the roles and
expectations of everyone is changing dramatically. The
answer to this confusion is very unclear, and therefore
different with almost every inclusion model.

First, let's highlight some characteristics of our model. I have been involved in a full time inclusion program with the same two regular education teachers for five years now. Naturally, the model you see today is not the one you would have seen back then. Our program has evolved over time and taken the shape it has today. The structure of our unit is as follows:

I teach in a sixth grade full inclusion unit. That means we have up to twelve identified students in our class. These students can be of any classification, including, developmentally disabled, learning disabled, emotionally disabled and other disabilities. The rest of the class consists of regular education students that the computer pumps out. These students are not hand selected; they represent the makeup of any other group of regular education students. Therefore, within the regular education group we have students who range from below to above grade level. We have had as many as thirty-two students total in the class. However, when our class total was around twenty-five, all our students were more successful.

Without Karen Finnegan and Kim Hugh, two highly capable staff, this inclusion program would not be what it is today.

Karen previously worked with special needs students in a self-contained classroom. She saw the difficulties with this environment and as a regular education teacher was open to sharing an inclusion unit with me. She didn't have to accept this challenge, but she did. Her attitude led us to the place we are today.

Kim was a new teacher, just out of college, when we started working together. She was open and excited about being in the classroom. She had participated in a trial inclusion unit during student teaching and had learned volumes which she brought with her into our classroom. Kim is young and excited about teaching and this shows in her work. Her concern for all students also helped make this program what it is today.

Initially, our inclusion program was more structured, and we spent lots of time meeting, planning, discussing and sharing ideas and concerns. As time has passed, we've come to know

I teach in a sixth grade full inclusion unit. That means we have up to twelve identified students in our class. These students can be of any classification of disability. The rest of the class consists of regular education students. They are not hand selected; they represent the makeup of any other group of regular education students.

each other better, and have become good friends. We know and accept each other's strengths and weaknesses in the classroom and we capitalize on them. We are together every day, all day, so that gives us the opportunity to fine tune our relationship. As I have heard many inclusion teachers say over and again, building a good "team" relationship takes time. The only way the team is going to grow, is if they are given the opportunity to do so and that takes years of working together. As time goes on, both staff and parents come to see us as a team and know they can speak with either of us on any issue involving any student that may be developing in our classroom.

Kim Hugh and Eileen Bowers

When the three of us began working together, we needed time to get to know one another as people and as professionals. To any special education teacher beginning a team teaching relationship, consider this; you are going into a classroom which for years has been another teacher's territory. By nature, we are territorial. In order to make this relationship work, proceed cautiously. In time, this will become your shared classroom, but initially it is her classroom and you are in her room supporting her. This is an uncomfortable spot for both of you. It will get better. Be as unintrusive as possible. Sit back, watch both the students and the teacher and observe what is going on around you. At the same time, pay attention to her teaching style. What techniques do you use that are compatible with her style? Make a note of them because you can use them to assist your students later on. Many special education students need to be taught how to learn in this environment. Techniques you are using to help yourself may be valuable to your students in time. In a sense, you are learning how they learn so that you can share this information with them. Additionally, pay attention to this teacher's teaching style. Learn how she teaches so you can explain this style to your students. For example, many

Building a good "team" relationship takes time. The only way the team is going to grow, is if it is given the opportunity to do so and that takes years of working together.

middle school teachers write notes on the board and ask students to copy them. That is a straightforward approach. Students do what they are told. However, there are other middle school teachers who do not write everything on the board. They repeat themselves over and again warning their students that if they are repeating themselves that means the information is important and they should be writing it down. This approach would need to be "taught" to most special needs students. In time, when you have joined her in the front of the room, you could be the one who writes the notes on the board while she instructs the class. Spend this time thinking about how the students are learning, how the teacher is teaching and where you can fit into this teaching/learning environment. You will find your spot. Once you have found a way to fit in, in a way to help the teaching process in the class, discuss this with your partner teacher. Share with her what you have observed and what that observation has shown you. Share with your partner teacher things you thought she did really well. Compliment her on her teaching. After all, how often do any of us hear those kind of remarks? Building this kind of rapport helps to strengthen the relationship. Over time, a strong relationship can withstand and accept constructive criticism in a healthy style.

By nature we are social beings. It's fun to work with someone else! I find myself laughing at things that happen and enjoying my work much more than I did when I taught alone.

Above all remember that you are two professional adults trying to help all of your students become the best people they can become. You are both responsible for the learning of all the students in the room, and as professionals, are responsible for complimenting and disciplining all of them. You are responsible for noticing and pointing out to your partner any observations you may make about any student, be it positive or negative. A good inclusion team is comparable to a good parenting relationship. You would never dream of having Dad in charge of the boys and Mom in charge of the girls. Both parents are responsible for all children. In a team teaching situation, things are no different. Learn to trust each other. Your partner teacher will inevitably do things differently than you. That's just fine. Respect each other's differences. Be flexible! This is a characteristic all

teachers should have. Working with children requires us to be flexible. Our best made plans often go awry. Learn how to roll with things. Flexibility lends itself to all kinds of new ideas. Some of these will work, some will not. But we will never know unless we are willing to try. Last but not least, enjoy each other. By nature we are social beings. It's fun to work with someone else! I find myself laughing at things that happen and enjoying my work much more than I did when I taught alone. After having been lucky enough to share my day with other professionals, I would never want to go back into a classroom alone. How long and boring that day would be!

We have worked out a unique form of disciplining in our classroom. Whenever either one of us notices a child misbehaving to the degree that he needs "a talking to" we talk to him together. If possible, we will take him out into the hall and talk about his behavior. If we can't take time out of class to do this we will ask him to stay after class and speak with him together. The point is that from the very beginning we show our students that we are a team. Whatever Kim or Karen tell our students, I will back it up. There are times that we have students try to play one of us against the other, but as soon as we figure that out, we make it clear that is unacceptable behavior in our room. The student will receive double trouble the next time that happens. Most students don't usually try that a second time.

Additionally, we hold all parent conferences together. If a parent calls the conference or if it is a scheduled parent conference, all three of us are present. I suppose that for some parents this may be overwhelming at first. However, we try to convey a very open, caring attitude toward their child and it generally puts most parents at ease right away. We try not to make a big deal about who are the special and who are the regular education teachers. We present ourselves as their child's teachers. Some parents do ask specific, pointed questions and we answer honestly. Overall, we are three professional teachers working with their children in the best way we know how.

We hold all parent conferences together. If a parent calls the conference or if it is a scheduled parent conference, all three of us are present.

What does a typical day look like? With up to twelve identified students and randomly selected regular education students, this group is together all day, traveling to various classes as a unit. That is true for all our sixth-grade classes, therefore, the inclusion unit "looks" no different than any of our other classes. As the special education teacher, I travel with them all day long as well. Our day begins in homeroom where Kim and I conduct the necessary home room duties. Both our name plates are above the classroom door and we refer to it as "our room." We have our own desks in it, hers in one corner and mine in the other. On any given day, one of us takes the lead in taking roll, and attending to homeroom duties. More often than not both of us are doing different things at the same time. All the students accept both of us as their teachers and will come to either of us during homeroom to have their many problems solved. It looks like two teachers doing one job, very efficiently.

When the first period bell rings we move right into English. On paper, Kim is in charge of the curriculum and I am in charge of applying modifications to the curriculum, but those duties have evolved as well. It is crucial that both the teachers be seen as teachers, and not one be seen as an assistant. A good coteaching partnership is like a good parenting partnership, with the child at the center of the relationship. That is, in fact, how we present ourselves to our students. For the most part, during English class, I am in

There are times that we have students try to play one of us against the other. As soon as we figure that out, we make it very clear that that is unacceptable behavior in our room.

On one occasion, a parent and her child came to a conference and asked to be removed from our class because they believed it was the "slow class." The parent felt the child was advanced and was somehow misinformed on the "pace" of learning in our classroom. We explained in detail what we were doing and how we were trying to accomplish it. We invited the child to sit in on another class in our unit to see if it was any different. We told them both that if they felt there was a great difference and they wanted to change classes, we would not hold them back. This student took us up on that offer, came back to us and said she was wrong. The class she visited was no different from ours. They were doing the same work we were and she liked the way we did it better. She went on to become a member of the National Junior Honors Society and had a very successful year. Her mom thanked us at the end of the year for being open to her questioning. She said her daughter grew tremendously that year and much of it came from the diversified group of learners she was with.

charge of the grammar part of the lesson and Kim is in charge of writing. We switch off on the spelling part of the lesson. These roles are not written in stone, however. It's important for both teachers to know what is going to be covered in all areas of the lesson so that one can cover for the other at any given time. If Kim gets called out of the room for anything and she is in the middle of teaching the writing piece, I jump in and continue where she left off. On the other hand, Kim makes it her job to learn the various needs of the identified students so that she can fill in for me at any time as well. We look upon it as team teaching. She brings certain assets to our classroom and I bring another set. There are no lines drawn defining "her students" and "my students." We are two teachers working with a classroom full of students, and they all win from this kind of team approach. Not only is it good for their learning experience, it adds to their social development. They see us modeling cooperation and coexistence. They see two adult professionals working together, having fun, accomplishing great things and respecting one another all at the same time. To me, this lesson is priceless. If all our children could learn to live this concept, what a wonderful world it would be.

We try not to make a big deal about who is the special and who is the regular educator, we just present ourselves as their teachers.

After English class, our students leave the room and go to their assigned study hall somewhere else in the building. We use this time to pull certain children — be they special or regular education students — out of study hall to receive extra tutoring on something they are struggling with, to take a test they missed, or to retake a test they messed up on. This is our time to provide any and all of our students with that little extra that helps take them over the top. At this time we may conduct some peer tutoring. At other times, we may not keep any students in at all. It depends who needs what and when.

A good coteaching partnership is like a good parenting partnership, with the child at the center of the relationship.

Following study hall students come back to our room for Reading. As a special education teacher, I have become fairly efficient in helping students develop a love for Reading. Therefore, I am the lead Reading teacher. I plan and teach all the Reading lessons and Kim assists students throughout the lesson. This is good for me, for Kim and for the students. I could never imagine not having the opportunity to teach on a given day. I am a teacher and I love to teach. So for me this is great. Additionally, Kim gets to watch another teacher and learn new techniques. And finally, the students get the opportunity to see both of us as teachers. Because of my background, I tend to set up my lessons in such a way that the special education students will be successful. We follow the same curriculum that all sixth-grade reading teachers follow and hold our students to the same set of standards. We just go about it a little differently. Kim uses these same lesson plans when she teaches reading to her other class later in the day.

After reading comes lunch. This is a great opportunity for the three of us to talk not only to each other about what is going on in our room but also with the other sixth grade teachers to see if they are experiencing the same things in their classrooms. The funny thing is, the problems or difficulties we are experiencing in the inclusion classroom are no different from those in the other sixth grade classrooms. This reemphasizes our point that they are all just children, with many of the same trials and tribulations, regardless of disability or a lack of one.

Following lunch we go back to our classroom and have Social Studies class. Kim enjoys teaching it and has come to perfect it over the years, so she takes the lead. As in all our classes, while Kim is teaching, I may interject something into the lesson that may be beneficial, or Kim and I will bounce things off each other. This enhances their learning experience and keeps things from getting dull. It's boring for students to listen to the same teacher lecture over and over again. The "team" approach helps break the monotony.

We work on an eight period day, with Social Studies fifth. Up to this point our inclusion class has been together for most of the day (with the exception of study hall and lunch). Sixth period is the time of day when we move together across the hall to Karen's classroom for Math and Science. This is a class where it's helpful to have two teachers circulating the room helping students individually with their work. We use the

I could never imagine not having the opportunity to teach in a given day. I am a teacher and I love to teach. So for me this is great. Additionally, Kim gets to watch another teacher and learn new techniques.

Saxon Math Book and it has very structured guided lessons so the planning takes care of itself. However, the style in which to teach the concept can vary. Traditionally, Karen will start the lesson out. I will interject ideas and if we feel the students are not getting it I may jump in and try another approach. Over the years we have figured out who can teach which concepts the best and that's how we do it. I may say to Karen, "I really like the way you explain negative numbers," so she will teach that lesson. In turn, she may say she likes the way I teach improper fractions, so I will teach that. There is a great deal of flexibility in this classroom because Math lends itself to that type of environment. There are different ways to teach different concepts and each year our students seem to be different from the ones before. Team teaching this class is fun and exciting.

After Math our students go to specials, such as art and gym, and return to Karen's class for Science. Karen is much more knowledgeable in Science than I am so she takes the lead here and I assist her and our students in whatever ways possible. During this class, while she is teaching, I have the opportunity to observe students and how they are learning. I am able to circulate and assist students individually at their own desks. I am also able to assist students in staying on track and keeping themselves focused on the lesson. This is great for our ADD students who tend to let their minds wander during abstract subjects like Science. Again, in Karen's room I have a desk in the back of the room with all my Math and Science materials available.

Whoever you talk with, the same questions concerning inclusion seem to be repeated over and again. Professionals all over the country are struggling with the same challenges while trying to implement an inclusion unit. We have wrestled with many of these questions and would like to share some of the conclusions we have arrived at through the years.

The funny thing is, the problems or difficulties that we are experiencing in the inclusion classroom are no different from those in the other sixth grade classrooms.

How do general and special educators decide how to share responsibilities?

When we first presented this question to our administrator, her response was simple. She said that on paper, the general educator was responsible for the curriculum and the special educator was responsible for modifying that curriculum for the students who needed it. This makes a great springboard. If you and your partner are new to inclusion, start here but don't end here. If you limit yourself to this structure, you are cutting off some great things that could happen in your classroom. As you become comfortable with each other, begin honest dialogue. Talk with one another honestly. Take risks. After having been in the classroom for a while as a special educator, you will have many ideas that may make a particular lesson, or unit, more exciting. Present them to your partner in an honest, nonthreatening way. Be willing to admit your strengths and weaknesses for the good of the students in your class. Allow the stronger teacher in each particular area to take the lead. Lean on each other for individual strengths. Help one another. Be willing to go that extra mile, grade that extra paper, plan that extra lesson if it will help your partner teacher. Stay open and be honest with each other through dialogue. Remember, the biggest regrets are over things not said.

Be willing to admit your strengths and weaknesses for the good of the students in your class and allow the stronger teacher in each particular area to take the lead.

How are disruptive behaviors dealt with and are they the sole responsibility of the special educator?

This question implies that the disruptive student is going to be the special education student. In my experience, the majority of times I have not found this to be the case. Regardless, when any student is being disruptive and interfering with the learning of others, he is not permitted to remain in the classroom. If he needs to be removed, then the instructor not teaching at the time is the one to do the removal. It's always a good idea to have a plan set in place for this type of situation. There should be a designated place — in coordination with the administrator — where disruptive students are sent when they need to be removed from the classroom. This, in my experience, is an extreme situation to be avoided when possible. The majority of behavior problems are better handled in the classroom. We have found that the best way to do this is to take that child out into the hall and speak to him individually. During the middle school years, teachers must be careful not to embarrass students in front of their peers. They must also be careful not to draw too much attention to the misbehaving student because in many cases that is exactly what he wants. Rather, we have found it best to handle it privately. As a rule, we (both) take him out to the hall and discuss what is going on. It is no different than when Mom and Dad speak to their misbehaving child together. This presents to the child the "team" approach we are trying to model. We have found this approach to be very successful. First of all, we don't "yell" at him so, he has no need to be defensive. We talk with him, ask him what is going on and explain why it can't be tolerated. This is usually enough. The total dialogue takes no more than two or three minutes. If more time is needed, we ask him to stick around after class, or make other arrangements to get together with him and discuss it. We have found that if we discuss things with children of middle school age respectfully, they will respond favorably. This approach seems to be successful with all children. There are occasions when a child will need a time out and we have those arrangements set in place ahead of time.

When any student is disruptive and interfering with the learning of others, he is not permitted to remain in the classroom. If he needs to be removed, then the instructor not teaching at the time does the removal.

Should the special educator work with the general education students in the class and vice versa?

A resounding yes! You are both teachers and your students are all students. As team teachers, you are responsible for the students in your classroom. Good team teaching is comparable to good parenting. Both are responsible for all aspects of all their children's behavior and performance. In a team teaching situation, things are no different. Once you draw lines in the sand, allowing certain teachers to do only

certain things with certain students, you sabotage your program. You want your program to grow and evolve over time and you restrict this by drawing such boundaries.

Also, the underlying force behind inclusion is to have students with special needs participate, both socially and academically, within the general population. If you limit the special education teacher to only work with special needs students in the inclusion model, you segregate those students within the general population. When you present yourself as a "team" and work with all students, there is no segregation taking place. You simply improve the teacher-student ratio and allow all students to become winners.

Are all students to be included, no matter what their individual behavioral or academic needs?

This is a controversial question and will be debated for quite some time. However, it has been my experience that the simple answer is no! The spirit of IDEA was meant to ask educators to look at each child individually. We are asked to consider every child's participation within the general population. If it's not a successful placement, we must justify that position. Not all children will benefit from a regular education classroom placement. I feel that it's an injustice to place some students in inclusive classrooms. We must put the child's needs first and ask ourselves where her needs can best be served. For many that is in the general population, but for some, it's not.

Schools are not supposed to be about teachers. Teachers are there to serve the children. Whatever is best for that child is what should be done, not what is best for the teacher.

For example, let's say we were deciding placement for a developmentally disabled child functioning three to four years below grade level. Maybe this child was chronologically entering the sixth grade but his reading and math skills were on a second grade level. Could we realistically think he would benefit from a sixth grade general education reading and math class? Most likely that child needs to learn functional skills like reading the clock, counting money, making change, reading functional signs, etc. Would we service this child efficiently if we placed him in a regular education sixth grade class? Those concepts wouldn't be covered in a sixth grade classroom and that child would need to be pulled out to learn them. However, she could be included in a general education class for art, music, gym, etc. As professionals, we need to look individually at each child and focus on her needs. Once her needs are established through objective and thorough testing, placement can best be decided. IDEA only asked that the general curriculum be the first placement considered. It was not presented as the "only" option for all children.

Why are some special educators, who clearly feel uncomfortable about inclusion, allowed to continue pull-out programs?

In my opinion, this is a huge injustice. Schools are not supposed to be about teachers. Teachers are there to serve the children. Whatever is best for that child is what should be done, not what is best for the teacher. I'm not trying to underestimate the difficulty we adults have accepting change. But the key word here is "adults." Adults are expected to fill the needs of children. That is our role. Any change is uncomfortable, but inevitable. Schools need to do what is best for kids! Administrators need to be able to rely on teachers to do just that.

During the middle school years, teachers must be careful not to embarrass students in front of their peers. They must also be careful not to draw too much attention to the misbehaving student because that is often what he wants.

How do you deal with general educators who are resistant to inclusion and constantly seek to sabotage it?

There is no easy answer to this one. This is a question for an administrator. It's important to make clear that successful inclusion programs exist in buildings where the administrator believes in and supports them. I was fortunate enough to be in such a situation. It was clearly understood by all staff members that our principal believed in introducing inclusion models into our school. I was lucky enough to be in there

when inclusion was introduced. First of all, we began an inclusion model before it became mandatory by law. Our principal brought the staff together, told us about this new program and how she saw it working out. She then asked the special education staff to select eight to twelve eighth-grade students with special needs who we thought would do well in the general curriculum. I guess you would call this selective inclusion. She then placed a young, vivacious special education teacher with these students. It was set up for success. Needless to say, the program was received well among the general education teachers. Showing the staff how this program could be successful helped put their fears to rest. There were lots of kinks that needed to be worked out over time but being proactive helped our building gain the upper hand. Over the years, we have gone from one inclusion model in the eighth grade to six inclusion models total, two in each of the three grade levels.

If you limit the special education teacher to working only with special needs students in the inclusion model, you segregate those students within the general population.

How are inclusion and coteaching implemented in smaller districts where there are limited resources?

Our district is medium-sized with a decent amount of funds, but we still need to watch expenses. We have three middle schools in our district. What we have done on this level — and it seems to be effective — is to have a large number of students with special needs sent to our building. That way we are allotted a larger number of special education teachers. That allows us to offer the full continuum of services in our own building. This type of population gives us the luxury of having two teachers in one inclusive classroom all day long. This makes it more cost effective and more advantageous for the students.

The alternative would be to have these students go to their home school. With students spread throughout the district, the special educator would have to travel throughout the week from building to building, meaning that students wouldn't have a special educator working directly with them in the classroom every day. She would serve more as a consultant to the regular education teacher than as a primary instructor in the classroom on a regular basis.

Once you draw lines in the sand, allowing certain teachers to do only certain things with certain students, you sabotage your program.

2

Why Try Inclusion?

As suggested by Kukic (1994), the debate on inclusion is emotional because it is truly a value-laden concept. Making inclusion work is based on a belief system that schools are for all children. The goal of inclusion, according to the Utah Agenda is, "to empower each student to becoming a caring, competent and contributing citizen in an integrated, changing, diverse society."

What is Inclusion?

Inclusion is not a place, it's a shared value, and one which promotes a single system of education to insure that all students become successful adults (Kukic, 1994). Inclusive education reflects a belief that all children are accepted members of the school community. It focuses on success and abilities, instead of failure and disabilities. In an effort to clarify terms, the inclusion discussed in this book rests on a coteaching model where both the regular and special educator work side by side serving disabled and non-disabled children within the general curriculum in the regular education classroom on a daily basis.

Research has been done regarding the ability of general education to effectively respond to the learning needs of the child with special needs. Is this the answer they have been looking for? The advantages of the coteaching model have been carefully examined. Not only does it promote learning for disabled and low achieving non-disabled students, it provides benefits for the professional (Walsh, 1992). Some studies also indicate teacher benefits come from the coteaching model, such as increased job satisfaction, increase in teaching/learning potential and enhanced stability. Results have shown that students involved feel less stigmatized socially, and they note overall parental satisfaction when compared to the "pull out" method (Madge, 1990).

The inclusion model discussed in this book rests on a coteaching model where both the regular and special educator work side by side serving disabled and non-disabled children within the general curriculum in the regular education classroom on a daily basis.

Why Consider Inclusion?

Part of the growth process is the phenomenon of learning. As individuals and as professionals, we are always looking for new ways to improve our lives and if possible, the lives of others.

In an article in Counterpoint entitled "Parents: A Typical Classroom is the Only Choice," parents of a child with Rett Syndrome share their story. When their child turned five, the parents began their search for a school. In this search the mother went to a special class first. After she left it, she said she felt stifled herself. There were no colored ABC's on the wall, no calendar on the board and no flag in the corner. She did not leave anxious to send her child there. Later in her search she visited a typical class where children were integrated at an early age. Overall she found, it was a more stimulating environment. After leaving this setting she was excited about her daughter's start of school. Reflecting back over the last ten years, she shared a couple of her thoughts. When students with cognitive disabilities "age out" of school

there are no self-contained malls or disability-friendly barber shops for them to go to. She felt her daughter's progress in the area of self-help and communication skills helped prepare her for life after school. She attributed a large piece of this progress to the fact that her daughter was around typical children and modeled her behavior after theirs. Her behavior improved dramatically and studies show that kids learn better from peers than adults.

How Does Inclusion Work?

Inclusion has as many different faces as those implementing it. As a rule, general teachers are in charge of curriculum and content, while special educators oversee the total programming, initiate modified activities, make curriculum adaptations and create classroom alternatives.

A special educator needs to walk with trepidation. She needs to respect her coteacher's space and understand her fears. Flexibility on the part of both teachers will lead all parties to success in this environment.

How Do Regular Education Students Benefit From Inclusion?

A parent activist group known as the Upside of Downs put on a seminar in December of 1990 in Cleveland. Their primary objective was to explain inclusive education to a group of professionals. As one of those in attendance, I left the conference with very mixed emotions. As a special educator, I was determined this was the way to go. But as a parent of "regular kids" I thought, "this sounds great but don't put students with special needs in my child's class because it will slow to a halt and we will lose out." Boy was I wrong!

As pointed out by Ro and Joe Vargo, the two parents that wrote the article in Counterpoint, Inclusion has positive effects on typical children. They will be the future caregivers, employers, neighbors, and parents of people with disabilities.

Inclusion helps typical children become more sensitive. Sensitivity is a value learned only through living. It's not something that can be taught. But it could be shared and expanded on in our society today.

To dispel some misconceptions about Inclusion, lets look at five myths discussed in an article published by the National Association of State Boards of Education:

Myth #1:

All special education students will be in a regular education program all the time.

NO. First of all, decisions will be made individually and take into effect individual strengths and weaknesses. Secondly, special education is not a place. It is a service that provides a continuum of options of which inclusion is just one.

Myth #2:

Inclusion is required by IDEA.

NO. IDEA simply speaks to the need for the least restrictive environment (LRE), while acknowledging that placement in a regular classroom cannot always be done satisfactorily.

Myth #3:

We will no longer need special education teachers.

NO. Inclusion is not mainstreaming. Inclusion depends on the support of a special education teacher, while mainstreaming calls on the regular teacher to "go it alone."

Myth #4:

Special education teachers will be aides in regular education classrooms.

NO. Special education teachers and regular educators learn to work together in a collaborative way. This collaboration depends on what is acceptable and comfortable for both teachers. A successful effective inclusion team can be compared to a strong parenting team; neither one dominates the other. This relationship should take on a collegial perspective. Two individuals share a similar body of knowledge or interest and feel free to engage in conversation to share ideas and jointly solve problems.

Myth #5:

Inclusion is a cost saving effort.

NO. According to John Herner, Director of Division of Special Education, inclusion was born out of the philosophy that all students have the right to a free, appropriate, public education (FAPE) with their peers; not an outgrowth of fiscal management concerns.

Let us now turn our attention to some present day contradictions in our current system; Mission statement vs. practices implemented.

As pointed out by Richard Schattman, EDS, in his chapter entitled "Supervisory Union: A Case Study of an Inclusive School System" there are contradictions in our present system.

First of all, most schools have mission statements that address the needs of all students, not just some. But in practice the educational emphasis seems to be on a limited number of students.

Secondly, most schools have mission statements proclaiming that education should enhance, not diminish, feelings of self worth. If you are separating a particular group, confirming by your actions they are too slow to function with other students — in some cases they can't ride the same bus or go to the same school — how does this enhance their self worth?

Third, most mission statements address appropriate development of social skills. How can this be accomplished when appropriate role modeling is not made available to the population that needs it the most?

As educators we know some modalities by which we learn are more dominant than others. But, in reality, we teach to one modality. Could it be that some students classified as learning disabled are not disabled at all? Maybe it has to do with the modalities we have used in our teaching. Maybe it's not their learning but our teaching that is disabled.

Eventually they will leave the safety of our shelter and be challenged to function in the work-a-day world. In school we dismissed them from difficult tasks, but the real world won't dismiss them from anything.

Looking at these contradictions, we have three options. We could modify the mission statement to address some students, but not all. We could change the section pertaining to student self worth and learn to accept less appropriate social skills from some students. We could ignore the differences between our mission statements and our practices. Or we could change our practice to better meet our mission statement, i.e., inclusion.

In order to make inclusion successful, we need to make changes in the way we think. As educators we know there are different modalities by which we learn, some more dominant than others. But, in reality, we teach to one modality. Could it be that some students classified as learning disabled aren't disabled in at all? Maybe it has to do with the traditional modalities we have used in our teaching. Maybe it's not their learning but our teaching that is disabled.

Secondly, we need to make some changes at the top — beginning with the universities. This is where pre-service teachers learn they are able to teach only a certain kind of student rather than developing a unified commitment to teach all students. Efforts need to be made on the part of higher education to consider what content is properly defined as specialized expertise and what is important for all teachers, regardless of the "kind of students they will be teaching."

By segregating children with handicapping conditions we are sending mixed messages to our entire student population. By putting them in separate rooms, giving them a separate curriculum, excusing them from national and state wide tests, we are saying, "you aren't responsible for doing difficult tasks that others have to do." Then, as they get closer to graduation we panic and say they're not ready, and they probably aren't. So our answer is to keep them in school longer. And we do. But all we're doing is postponing the inevitable because they eventually leave the safety of our shelter and are challenged to function in the work-a-day world. In school we dismissed them from difficult tasks, but the real world won't dismiss them from anything. They still have to read the driver's test to get a license, fill out an application to get a job, understand insurance policies, mortgages and tax returns. Our empathy for their disabilities works much like people who enable a "beloved alcoholic." Rather than teaching him ways to live with his condition, we, as enablers, make excuses for him. We cover up whenever necessary and clean up after they fall. This only gives them permission to continue their lifestyle. This is not unlike "special services" we provide to children with disabilities. Rather than teaching a child who can't do math how to use a calculator, or a child who can't spell how to use a spell check program, or a child who can't write how to work a simple computer, we dismiss him from age appropriate material and give him work below the level of his peers. The message we are sending comes across loud and clear, "you can't do this hard work and you don't have to." It then becomes a self-fulfilling prophecy. They told me I am stupid, I'll act stupid. They told me I was a behavior problem, I'll be a behavior problem. They told me I don't have to do hard work, so I won't. Then, as special educators we spend 75% of our day working on building up their self esteem. Let's try not to shatter it in the first place. Being in a self contained classroom for a number of years, I got questions like, "are we going to graduate and get a 'tard' diploma, or do we not get one at all?" "Will our diploma say 'retarded student?' " These questions rip at the heart of special educators and we spend the rest of the year trying to dispel these perceptions. Too often we are unsuccessful.

The disadvantages of a separate special education program outweigh advantages. Schools are places to prepare our children for the real world. Removing handicapped children does not accomplish that. Individuals with disabilities are members of our society. The time to include them is now. Inclusion is an avenue to ending the discrimination of students with disabilities. Maybe it will usher in a rebirth of empathy that seems to be so lacking in our society today. The positive effects of inclusion will be felt by many people, not just a few.

The message we are sending comes across loud and clear, "you can't do this hard work and you don't have to."
It then becomes a self-fulfilling prophecy.

3

Whose IDEA is this Anyway?

IDEA Reauthorization

In 1975 when PL 94-142 was first introduced, it changed the face of the public school population. As we know today, this has continued to evolve, causing a widening ripple of change in the way our schools are run and the way we serve students.

Prior to '75 many special education students were not even receiving an education or got it in a separate facility, often at the expense of their parents. PL 94-142 changed all that and loudly stated that all children, including those with special needs were entitled to a free, appropriate, public education. Of course the law stated much more, but the "free, appropriate, public education" was the aspect schools initially concentrated on. At this time, the public school doors were open to the special education population. But as we all know, these kids were often not seen by others. They were in the "special education room" in the far corner of

If the student was thought able to handle the curriculum of a regular class, he was given that material in the resource room and his progress was monitored. At the okay of the regular educator, he would enter the room. He was left to his own resources and was expected to carry the load of the regular curriculum. If he couldn't do this, he was sent back to the resource room.

some long hallway. They were permitted to eat with the regular education population, but since no one knew them, they stuck to themselves and didn't mingle with the general population. It was assumed by school personnel, including the special educator, that they would be educated in special education rooms unless they could prove they were "able" to hold their own in a regular education classroom. If it was decided that a special education student might be able to handle the curriculum of a particular regular education class, he was first given that material in the resource room and his progress was monitored for a few weeks. At the okay of the regular education teacher, that child would enter the room. He was left to his own resources and was expected to carry the load of the regular education curriculum. If he couldn't do this, he was sent back to "the resource room."

The assumption was that he was to be educated in the resource room unless we could justify why he should be in the general curriculum.

Civil Rights movements and legislation like Americans with Disabilities Act (ADA) began to heighten awareness of disabled persons in this country. Parents joined the movement and began to form advocacy groups. Some very active parent groups spearheaded these discussions with parents, professionals and government officials. These groups demanded that their voices be heard.

The least restrictive environment provision of the law states that children with disabilities must be educated with non-disabled peers to the maximum extent possible with necessary supports provided. The LRE provision was part of the law because separate education is not equal as seen in the Supreme Court decision of 1954 (Brown vs. the Board of Education) which states, "in the field of public education, the doctrine of 'separate but equal' has no place."

However, because of intense efforts to implement PL 94-142 fully, a "special" and separate education system evolved with the assumption that to have their needs met, students with disabilities are best served in segregated settings. In the process of implementing the letter of the law (that students are entitled to education), the spirit of the law (that children have the right to learn together) was lost.

It's important to note that mainstreaming and inclusion are not mandated by PL 94-142 or IDEA. However, educating students in the least-restrictive environment is an integral component of the law. Both these placement options are within the definition of the least-restrictive environment. It's important to point out that mainstreaming and inclusion are just that, placement options. When deciding on educational placements, it's important for educators to realize that inclusion is the least-restrictive environment. If it meets the student's needs. Otherwise self-contained settings are viable alternatives. The key is that placements meet the students' needs.

Educators must remember to center on the child when deciding on a placement within the continuum of services. Although inclusion may "feel nice," it's mandatory that we look at responsible inclusion. "Responsible inclusion" is the process of providing educational services for students with high-incidence disabilities in the general education classroom based on academic and social progress of the student. Its goal is to place all students in the general education classroom unless their academic and social needs can't be adequately met there. Thus, with responsible inclusion the academic and social progress of the student is continually monitored. If students are not making adequate progress, alternatives are considered. With responsible inclusion the responsibility is first and foremost to the student, not the educational programs or beliefs of the faculty in the school. We need to do what's best for all kids.

IDEA has brought with it a great push to have the parents serve as an equal partner in the team of professionals working with the child. For example, in the past the IEP was prepared by the teacher and presented to the parent as "the way it is" and signed off on by both parties. This is no longer the case. The parent is called and asked to participate ahead of time in the preparation of the IEP. Whenever possible, the parent and the teacher are supposed to sit down together to

Because of intense efforts to implement PL 94-142 fully a "special" and separate education system evolved, which assumed that to have their needs met, students with disabilities can best be served in segregated settings. In the process of implementing the letter of the law (students are entitled to education), the spirit of the law (they have the right to learn together) was lost.

construct the IEP for the child. Of course, this is difficult to work out logistically, but the fact remains that the parent has a much greater voice than ever before.

With any new change comes great confusion and varying individual interpretations. There is confusion in the new terminology and differences in the interpretation of both. Mainstreaming vs. inclusion is the biggest confusion in terminology. Mainstreaming was around long before IDEA came into effect. Mainstreaming was, and still is, a program that provides the opportunity to be educated with nondisabled children in the regular classroom. If it was felt by the IEP team that the child was functioning close to grade level, they may place him in a regular classroom for instruction. However, he went into the classroom alone and received little or no special education support while there. It was possible for the special educator to assist him with some work outside the classroom. That assistance was administered on a tutorial basis. For the most part, the child was held to the same set of standards and graded on the same grading system as everyone else in the classroom.

In the past the IEP was prepared by the teacher and presented to the parent as "the way it is," and both parties signed off. This is no longer the case. Today the parent is called and asked to participate ahead of time in the preparation of the IEP.

"Inclusion" is a program new to IDEA. This concept was born out of the '97 reauthorization. When attending the various inservices provided by parent groups this term was used universally. Their cry, "We want our children included," has been heard and acknowledged. The inclusion program differs from mainstreaming in that the child with special needs is taken out of the self-contained and placed in the regular classroom. In this program, the teacher goes with the identified children and services them along side the other students. Accommodations and modifications are made by the special educator to meet the needs of her students. The regular educator is the professional held responsible for teaching curriculum and the special educator is held responsible for adapting the curriculum. For the child, it's the best of both worlds. They are able to be part of the school population and not face total frustration in their academic work. Inclusion was addressed because it was the right thing to do. With further study, it was proven that the special needs child flourished in this environment. Greater

expectations were placed on them and they rose to the occasion. They showed improvement in social skills because they were surrounded by students who modeled normal, acceptable social skills. It was also believed that typical students would become more sensitive to people with special needs and that would add to our understanding as a society. Studies show that this, in fact, is becoming a reality. Studies also show that children normally considered "at risk" progress further in an inclusive classroom. To date, there is solid evidence that the regular education student can and does progress as far as expected in the inclusive classroom. Scores demonstrated in Chapter Six bring this evidence to light.

Inclusion was originally intended to allow children with special needs to stay at their home school and be taught with neighborhood peers. This does not seem to be playing out as it was intended. This is due to the finances involved in the set up. In order to implement inclusion effectively, a special educator must be present as close to 100% of the time as is possible. It has been proven that when we "team teach" the results are more successful than when the relationship is one of "consulting." Having the special needs teacher work directly with the child carries the highest success rate. In order to do this, children with special needs can't be spread throughout the district. As a result, many districts gather these children into one or two schools to provide service in an inclusive setting. This seems to be the most economical way to accomplish this goal.

Other confusing terminology includes "accommodations" and "modifications" to allow the child to participate in the general curriculum. This must be addressed in the IEP. Accommodations are supports or services provided to help a student access and demonstrate learning and modifications are changes made to the content and performance expectations. Modifications are a direct result of the child's handicapping condition. When exemption is given to proficiency tests it's usually stated that it is made because the child has been participating in a modified curriculum.

Inclusion was initiated because it was the right thing to do. Study has proven that the special needs child flourishes in this environment.

It was also believed that students would become more sensitive to people with special needs and that would add to our understanding as a society. Studies show this is becoming a reality.

In public schools, 95% of all exceptional children are placed in four categories: Learning disabled, speech and language impaired, mentally handicapped and emotionally disturbed. The "special" population in American public schools is now about 14 percent of all students.

I work very closely with the Special Education Curriculum Supervisor in our district in an effort to make this program as successful as possible. Of course, there are many factors involved. One key aspect must be in place to reach maximum success. When rating the most important one, we agreed it was the professionalism of the team teachers and their willingness to make this program successful. Not unlike good parenting, both need to know what the other is doing at any given moment. Each teacher should be able to fill in for one another when the opportunity presents itself. Each should respect the other's decisions in curriculum areas and with the students. Planning should be cooperative and paper work should be evenly divided. When both work cohesively with all students, success is bound to increase. If there is any aversion to each other or to the program, it's bound to come through no matter how hard you try to hide it. Unfortunately, when this is the case the students are the ones that lose.

Modifications in the curriculum can be numerous. They should serve as bridges to help the identified student make the leap from where he is functioning to the curriculum. For example, if in math class the majority of the work is presented in word problem format, the special educator can present some of it as calculation problems. The work can be modified in many ways. The teacher can modify the work in its presentation form as described above. Or, it can be modified in the grading. The special educator may be looking for something altogether different in a written piece than is the regular educator. Or, the work can be modified in the scoring. The special educator may use a "handicap score" as in golf when a test calls for prior knowledge the child doesn't have. Or, the quantity of work can be modified. If the class is copying notes off the board or overhead, the special educator can provide some students with a skeletal outline with words deleted that need to be

One key aspect must be in place to reach maximum success: The professionalism of the team and its willingness to make the program successful. Not unlike good parenting, both need to know what the other is doing at any given moment.

filled in, rather than have them copy all the notes (e.g., if the student has a severe eye hand coordination difficulty). Or, the work can be modified in the assessment. If a child has difficulty reading, social studies and science tests could be read to him or administered orally. That way the content is assessed rather than the reading level of the student.

These are just a few of the many ways to modify and adjust the curriculum and they need to be made on an individual basis centered around the child's handicapping condition.

When implemented appropriately, this is the "Cadillac" of all special education programs. Like every educational program, inclusion is made up of great intentions. When administered correctly, it's an excellent program for many children. However, inclusion does not offer benefits to every special needs child. In addition, IDEA does not mandate all children to be in an inclusive program. It's just another program available on the continuum of services.

If a child can't be taught in a regular classroom, documentation must be made as to when, why and for what reason will that child be pulled. Gone are the days when we were permitted to "pigeonhole" children and put them in categories they can't escape from. Our society needs to be taught tolerance for people who look, act, talk and learn differently. We cannot teach all children in an inclusive classroom. This is where IQ's and other tests of basic skills, like the Brigance Inventory, come into play. Through the results of these tests, we make educated decisions on where this child will best learn and what he is in greatest need of learning. If a child scores around a 50-60 IQ and can't recognize emergency words, doesn't know how to use a telephone, or is lacking in other functional skills, then it would most likely be decided by the IEP team that he would be best served in a self-contained room. If however, the child scored somewhere around the 70 range, with modifications made to the curriculum he would be better served in a regular education classroom. Not only does this child receive academic stimulation, he also is provided with a group of children exhibiting normal social behaviors. People are social

Teachers should respect each other's decisions in curriculum areas. Planning should be cooperative and paper work should be evenly divided. When both are working cohesively with all students, success will increase. However, if there is any aversion to each other or to the program, it's bound to come through no matter how hard you try to hide it. Unfortunately, when this is the case the students are the ones who lose.

IDEA has not mandated that all children be educated in the general curriculum. It simply states that the least restrictive environment be considered on an individual basis. We must always keep our eye on what is best for the individual child.

learners in origin, making inclusion a better atmosphere for a child. Without the knowledge of his IQ score, however, we wouldn't know what level of expectation to impose on him. Also, testing supplies us with information about his learning modalities, his strengths and weaknesses and emotional components of his personality. These are great sources of information when assisting a child on his developmental path.

What about the regular education child in the inclusive classroom? Look at the golden opportunities he is being given. If administered correctly, the curriculum is not watered down at all. The regular education teacher continues to teach the class as she always has, same speed, same content, same expectations. The special educator is responsible for modifying the curriculum to meet the individual needs of the identified children. Can she help other "at risk" children at the same time? Absolutely! This is one of the benefits of the program. In this example, both groups of children come out the winner.

4

Practical Strategies for the Coteaching Classroom

Philosophy of the Coteaching Model

The goal of the coteaching or inclusive classroom is to make all children feel as though they belong and are as capable as everyone else. Ultimately, distinctions should not be made between special and regular education students. Therefore, modifications and accommodations need to be delivered with discretion. It's never good practice to say to a child, "you only have to do five problems and everyone else has to do ten." This creates bad chemistry for everybody. The students doing ten problems immediately resent the child doing five and this leads to social problems in the development of relationships which are often strained to begin with. In addition, we are sending the wrong message to the student with special needs. We are telling him that he is not capable of doing what everyone else has to do. This is not the right message. Rather, we want to tell these children they do have to carry their own weight. It's necessary for us as educators

Modifications and accommodations need to be delivered with discretion. It's never good practice to say to a child, "you only have to do five problems and everyone else has to do ten."

to make them aware of their disabilities and teach them how to live with and work around them. We must be careful not to enable or make excuses for them. As educators, we have the obligation to teach all children how to be successful functioning members of our society.

Self esteem is a huge piece of the success level of any student in the classroom. When implementing needed accommodations and modifications, don't forget you're handling a child who wants to be like everyone else and accepted as 'one of the group.' Walk gently and guard your task very carefully.

Accommodations vs. Modifications

Accommodations are supports or services provided to help a student access and demonstrate learning:	**Modifications** are changes made to student content and performance expectations:
• Skeletal set of notes	• Eliminate higher level questions
• Oral reading	• Grade curving
• Words on tape	• Not responsible for all learner outcomes

In our state, substantial modifications to the curriculum allow for students to be exempt from the high stakes of the Ohio Proficiency Test, accommodations do not!

Children who learn together, learn to live together.

Accommodations

Supports or services provided
to help a student access and demonstrate learning.

Assignment Initial Program

For students who have difficulty completing homework, this
accommodation helps tremendously. Whenever possible,
write the assignment on the board, and give it verbally as
well. After the student has written all of them in his
assignment book, instruct him to bring it to you. You then
check to make sure all assignments are written correctly.
It's helpful if the teacher keeps an assignment book of her
own so there is a source to refer to. When assignments are
not written correctly, instruct the student to "make your
assignment book look like mine." When assignments are
written correctly, initial the book. Teacher initials indicate
that all assignments are copied properly. If necessary, review
the books students need to get from their lockers. At home,
after the child has completed his homework, she is instructed
to show completed work to her parents. They are asked to
just check for completion, not for accuracy. When all
assignments are completed and accounted for, parent's initial
that the work was finished. This is established with them
prior to the implementation of the program. This program
provides just enough structure to hold the student
accountable for his work both at home and at school. It is
also advantageous for the student to see home and school
working as a team.

Assignments for the Week of _____

Subject	Assignment	Status

MONDAY

		☐
		☐
		☐
	← NO SCHOOL →	☐
		☐
		☐
		☐
		☐

TUESDAY

Subject	Assignment	Status
Eng.	final copy time mag. outline & rough draft.	☑
Read.	W.S.	☑
S.S	Impeachment----- (EB)	☑
Math	L59 (1-20)	☑
Sci.	Eclipse poster-due Friday.	☑
	Kim Smith	☐
		☐
		☐

WEDNESDAY

Subject	Assignment	Status
Eng.	Write 10 smilies	☐
Read.	Ch. 4-6 Holes, Pop W.S. #23-26 fact-opinion	☐
S.S	Govt. W.S. review Govt. test Fri.	☐
Math	L60	☐
Sci.	Eclipse poster due Fri.	☐
		☐
	Kim Smith (EB)	☐
		☐

The teacher's initials (EB) indicate the assignments are written correctly. The parent's signature (Kim Smith) indicates the assignments have been completed. Remember: Do not ask parents to check student work, just look for completion.

Color Code Spelling Words

If a student is a stronger visual than auditory learner, color coding spelling words can help him learn correct spelling. Instruct him to code each syllable with a different color. Have him study them by syllable and demonstrate this procedure for him. Show him how to color code the word, look at it on his paper, close his eyes and see it in syllables in his mind. Depending on the strength of this modality, this accommodation can be helpful.

1. patch

2. flash|back

3. grand|dad

4. knap|sack

5. depth

6. swept

7. wal|nut

8. them|selves

9. myth

10. fifth

Cooperative Learning

The Russian psychologist, Lev Vygotsky argues that all intellectual abilities are social in nature. Language and thought first appear in early interactions with parents, and continue to develop through contact with teachers and others. Some might argue that traditional intelligence tests ignore what Vygotsky call the "zone of proximal development." This is the difference between what a learner can accomplish independently and what he or she can accomplish with the guidance and encouragement of a more skilled partner. We incorporate this type of learning in school all the time when we encourage collaborative work among peers, cooperative learning or tutoring sessions to help assist

The "zone of proximal development" is the difference between what a learner can do independently and what she can accomplish with the guidance and encouragement of a more skilled partner.

a slower student. Vygotsky contends that children learn through social collaboration which fosters cognitive growth such as "scaffolding" or "guided participation." These are expert/novice and adult/child interactions in which students are shaped as they actively participate in culturally relevant activities working with skilled partners. This type of intellectual development has been around for a long time. It dates back to the days when we had apprentices working together in the skilled trades. The types of learning strategies that Vygotsky addresses, zone of proximal development, scaffolding and guided participation are all successfully used in school today. For example, a child rolls the dice in a board game. She stares at the teacher because she can't read the dice. Through modeling the teacher shows her how to count the dots on the dice and how to move her piece on the board. On the child's next turn, the teacher says, "count the dots on the dice." The student counts the dots and moves her piece. On subsequent turns, the child performs the activity on her own without being told or shown. These theories can be applied to any situation through cooperative learning.

Cooperative Learning is an accommodation that has proven helpful for all students in all subject areas. Provide opportunities for your students to work together. The struggling student can gain leaps and bounds when she is working with a peer. Studies show, however, that it is not advantageous to group high with low functioning students. When this takes place, the higher functioning student becomes frustrated and "takes over." This alienates the other student, who withdraws. So, play close attention to the pairing of students. Identified students will be more comfortable, and studies show they will work more successfully with an at-risk student. Of course, teacher intervention and assistance with this group will be paramount.

Cooperative learning is different from group work. In cooperative learning, students work together to learn or practice a particular concept or skill. Final assessment of how well this concept or skill was mastered is done individually.

High Points

- Students working with students.
- Matching identified students with at-risk students.
- Assess and grade students individually.
- Teacher intervention is necessary.

A student drawn picture of a cooperative learning situation.

To avoid frustration on either student's part, match them up based on ability. In the beginning of the year, I administer the Brigance Test of Basic Skills to get an overall reading level on each student in the entire class. I use the results to pair them for cooperative learning groups. For example, after administering the silent reading section of the Brigance Test, I learned the following information.

Susie Jones	functioning on a 6th grade level
Jimmy Masters	functioning on a 7th grade level
Sally Richards	functioning on a 5th grade level
Mike Ethers	functioning on a 4th grade level
Kristy Bauers	functioning on a 6th grade level
Josh Summers	functioning on a 4th grade level
Ellen Smith	functioning on a 5th grade level
Amy Brown	functioning on a 7th grade level

Working Partners

Susie Jones	and	Kristy Bauers
Jimmy Masters	and	Amy Brown
Sally Richards	and	Ellen Smith
**Mike Ethers	and	Josh Summers

**The teacher must pay close attention to this pair since they are functioning significantly below grade level. These students will need more teacher intervention than some of the other groups.

Develop Study Guides

This accommodation is a wonderful tool for all children, and can be used in all subject area content. Several days before the administration of a test, the special educator obtains a copy of the test from the regular educator. Using the test and student notes, construct a review sheet or a study guide. The guide can be given to the whole class to complete and use. Depending on how the partner teachers want to work it out, this guide can be an activity first, then used as a study guide, or it can be a list of curricula that should be studied in preparation for the test. Of course, if it is an activity and the students are filling in answers, either with other students or alone, the teacher must check answers for accuracy before studying for the test.

Several days before the administration of a test, obtain a copy of it from the regular educator. Use it to construct a study guide.

Study Guide

Chapter 3   Lesson 2

Vocabulary	Important Places, Ideas, Events, People
1. Agriculture: the raising of crops and animals for human use.	1. Catal Huyuk: one of world's first large cities found by archaeologists. Once housed 5,000 people.
2. New Stone Age: period from 12,000 yrs. ago to approx. 6,000 yrs. ago.	2. Agriculture brings change.
3. Domesticate: to train something to be useful to people.	3. Agriculture created a surplus.
4. Surplus: an extra supply of something.	4. Demands on farmers time brought about Specialization.
5. Specialization: people training to do a certain kind of work.	

Study Guide

Day/Date of Test: _____

Today's Date: _____

Day/Dates I plan to study: _____

List six main ideas about the topic:

1. _____
2. _____
3. _____
4. _____
5. _____
6. _____

List ten important vocabulary terms and their definitions that are related to topic:

1. _____
2. _____
3. _____
4. _____
5. _____
6. _____
7. _____
8. _____
9. _____
10. _____

List any other key concepts, people, places, important events, etc.:

1. _____
2. _____
3. _____
4. _____

Pretend you are the teacher. On the back, write 15 possible test questions.

Communicate

Home to School Communication

For a student who tends to have difficulty studying, this accommodation is helpful. It's good practice to announce tests several days in advance, a week if possible. When a test is announced, the special educator meets with the student to make sure he knows exactly what content is going to be tested. Then write a note in his assignment book to the parents requesting that they begin to assist their child in preparing for the test. Studying is a skill many students need to be taught. Often it's assumed that they know how to do it when it is not so. Have parents sign the note and instruct students to show you their signatures. This way you're ensured that the parent really is aware of the upcoming test.

High Points

- Announce test date a week in advance.
- Special educator meets with special education students.
- Help organize notes to study from.
- Notify parents of test in assignment book.
- Teach special education students study skills by modeling in study sessions.
- Repeat this practice until test date.

Locker Organization

For many students, survival in a middle school becomes a nightmare because they have no idea how to organize themselves, starting with their lockers. This is a skill that must be taught. If the special educator notices a child having difficulty bringing the correct supplies to class, she can help him set up his locker in an organized fashion. However, don't stop there. Once the locker is organized, the child may still have difficulty because he is not organized. If this is the case, have him bring the special educator all the material needed for the morning classes. If the teacher notices something is missing, take care of it then rather than disturbing class later on. The student is then instructed not to return to the locker until lunch time. If he does, he may mistakenly put away a needed item. If necessary, repeat this same procedure before lunch in preparation for afternoon classes.

High Points

- Teacher and student organize locker together.
- Morning books on the top shelf of the locker.
- Afternoon books on the bottom shelf.
- Student shows teacher morning materials in home room.
- Student shows teacher afternoon materials after lunch.
- Student visits locker only four times a day.
- Before home room, before lunch, after lunch and after school.

If the special educator notices a child having difficulty bringing correct supplies to class, she can help him set up his locker in an organized fashion.

A student drawn picture of a neat locker.

Oral Reading

This accommodation can be used in any of the subject areas. For many struggling students silent reading is a difficult task; oral reading helps them absorb material through listening skills. Some poor readers have excellent listening comprehension levels. In reading class, novels and stories can be read aloud. In content subjects, text can be read aloud. At times, the teacher can read text to the class. Other times student volunteers can read to the class. Or students can partner up with a reading buddy and read to each other. Again, remember not to pair high students with lower performing ones. Try to keep the ability gap between students somewhat close. Once reading is complete, discuss with the group what they read. Don't assume the text was properly comprehended. Regular and special educators must ensure that the main points were obtained. This may require a great deal of discussion before, during and after the reading. Encourage students to "draw a picture in their mind's eye" as they read along. Visualization is a reading strategy that can strengthen reading comprehension.

High Points

- Read text aloud in class.
- At times, teacher reads content to class.
- Other times, students read content to class.
- Other times, pair reading partners to read to each other.
- After reading, discuss or note-take important points.
- Teach visualization as a reading strategy to enhance comprehension.

Skeletal Set of Notes

As with many accommodations, this can be used in any subject area. However, it's primarily intended for Social Studies and Science. If the regular educator is going to put notes on the board, or an overhead, the special educator needs to obtain a copy of them ahead of time. She then can make a skeletal set. This set matches the notes that appear on the overhead. However, approximately 25 – 35% of the keywords and phrases have been omitted. When the note-taking activity begins in the class, the student is given one of these sheets. He is instructed to follow-along, inserting only keywords and phrases that have been deleted. It's easier for the student if the notes on the overhead are an identical match to those he's using. In fact, the special educator may want to type the set of notes that will be put on the overhead. This way, both overhead and skeletal set can be constructed at the same time and will produce an identical match.

Chapter 3   Lesson 2

I. **Agriculture**: the raising of crops and animals for human use

    A. The New Stone Age: The period beginning 12,000 years ago and ending roughly 6,000 years ago.

        1. Stone tools were still depended on, but people began experimenting with agriculture.

II. **Catal Huyuk**: One of the world's first cities. It is the largest city uncovered by archaeologist.
The city once housed about 5,000 people.

    A. Agriculture brings change.

        1. To use agriculture, people had to domesticate plants and animals.

            a. **Domesticate**: To train something to be useful to people.

    B. New Ways of Life

        1. Agriculture created a surplus.
            a. **surplus**: An extra supply of something.

        2. The demands on farmers time led to specialization

            a. **Specialization**: People training to do particular kinds of work.

Chapter 3   Lesson 2

I. Agriculture: the raising of _____.

    A. _____: the period beginning 12,000 years ago and _____.

        1. Stone tools were still depended on, but _____ _____.

II. Catal _____ – one of the world's _____.
  It is the _____.
  The city once housed about 5,000 people.

    A. Agriculture brings _____.

        1. To use agriculture, people _____ and _____.

            a. domesticate: _____.

    B. New Ways of Life

        1. Agriculture _____.
            a. _____: an extra supply of something.

        2. The _____ specialization.

            a. specialization: _____.

Chapter 3   Lesson 2

I. **Agriculture**: the raising of crops and animals for human use.

   A. The New Stone Age: The period beginning 12,000 years ago and ending roughly 6,000 years ago.

      1. Stone tools were still depended on, but people began experimenting with agriculture.

II. **Catal Huyuk**: One of the world's first large cities uncovered by archaeologists.

The city once housed about 5,000 people.

   A. Agriculture brings change.

      1. To use agriculture, people had to domesticate plants and animals.

         a. **Domesticate**: To train something to be useful to people.

   B. New Ways of Life

      1. Agriculture created a surplus.
         a. **surplus**: An extra supply of something.

      2. The **demands** on farmers time led to specialization.

         a. **Specialization**: People training to do particular kinds of work.

Chapter 3   Lesson 2

I. Agriculture: the raising of _____.

    A. _____: the period beginning 12,000

      years ago and _____.

        1. Stone tools were still depended on, but _____

        _____.

II. Catal _____ – one of the world's _____.

    It is the _____.

    The city once housed about 5,000 people.

    A. Agriculture brings _____.

        1. To use agriculture, people _____

        and _____.

          a. domesticate: _____.

    B. New Ways of Life

        1. Agriculture _____.

          a. _____: an extra supply of something.

        2. The _____specialization.

          a. specialization: _____.

Study Sessions

As mentioned, many struggling students do not know how to study correctly. The ideal situation is to work with them during study hall. If this is not possible, a before or after school session would work out. The special educator begins by modeling what is meant by "studying." She teaches the student how to review notes in preparation for a test or quiz. This skill is reinforced by working one-on-one with the student, assisting him in preparing for an upcoming test. The study skills taught here might carry over into study sessions some students are having with their parents. Ultimately, the goal is to teach the student how to study independently.

High Points

- Meet with students one-on-one or in small groups:
- Teacher uses student's copy of notes.
- Teacher models "how to study."
- Allow student to try while teacher watches.
- Teacher reinforces good study habits with student.

Words on Tape

This accommodation is intended to be used with spelling or vocabulary comprehension. However, you may find that it works in other areas as well. Often a child's listening comprehension is stronger than her reading comprehension. Encourage her to use this modality to study both vocabulary and spelling words. Here's how it works. The special education teacher models this for the student initially, but then she should be able to do this on her own at home. The student is instructed to read the spelling word into the tape recorder, leave a pause on the recorder and then spell the word into it a second time. He repeats this procedure for each word. For daily homework, the child is instructed to listen to the tape. During the pause, he spells the word aloud. Practice is repeated as much as is necessary. This same procedure can be followed for vocabulary words and their definitions.

Explaining this procedure to the parents may help make this activity more successful.

High Points

- Great for the auditory learner.
- Pronounce word into tape recorder.
- Spell word into tape recorder.
- Leave a pause.
- Repeat word and spell into tape recorder.
- Leave a second pause.
- Continue process for all listed spelling words.
- Once recorded, student listens to the tape repeating and spelling the word aloud during the pause.

Note: This procedure can be used when a student is studying vocabulary words as well. Just recite definition rather than the spelling of the word.

Written Spelling Tests

This type of spelling assessment can be given to the whole class if special and regular educator are in agreement. Dictated spelling tests often cause a great deal of anxiety for students who are poor spellers. Therefore, rather than a dictated test, a written one can be administered. There are two basic formats to the written tests. On one, spelling words are typed three different ways, one of which is correct. Students are asked to circle that word. On the second, students unscramble the spelling words. For these tests the teacher dictates the words, one by one. The student uses the scrambled letters on the page to spell the word.

The special educator can construct these tests using spelling lists already in place in the classroom. If both teachers decide not to use these tests for the whole class, they can be given to the students with special needs, or given as a make-up when students perform poorly on the first.

Spelling Test		
Name _____		Date _____
1. fifth	fefth	fivth
2. patsh	patch	pach
3. mith	mythe	myth
4. flash back	flashback	flachback
5. themselfs	themsefs	themselves
6. grandddad	granddad	grandadd
7. thred	thread	thraed
8. napsak	napsack	knapsack
9. swepp	swepted	swept
10. deeth	deebth	depth
11. sponge	spong	sponje
12. fringe	frenge	fring
13. wood chuck	woodchuck	woodchuk

Spelling Test		
Name _____		Date _____
1. domle	_____	because
2. lreotcean	_____	different
3. reeht	_____	interesting
4. aehr	_____	model
5. udnhdres	_____	really
6. eriht	_____	usually
7. uausyll	_____	favorite
8. frefidnet	_____	here
9. riitsp	_____	hear
10. ot	_____	there
11. reeh	_____	their
12. ternitsegni	_____	to
13. eitrovaf	_____	hundreds

Spelling Test

Name _____ Date _____

1. fifth   fefth   fivth

2. patsh   patch   pach

3. mith   mythe   myth

4. flash back   flashback   flachback

5. themselfs   themsefs   themselves

6. grandddad   granddad   grandadd

7. thred   thread   thraed

8. napsak   napsack   knapsack

9. swepp   swepted   swept

10. deeth   deebth   depth

11. sponge   spong   sponje

12. fringe   frenge   fring

13. wood chuck   woodchuck   woodchuk

14. glipse   glimpse   glimse

15. walnut   walnot   wallnut

Spelling Test

Name _____ Date _____

1. domle   _____ because

2. lreotcean   _____ different

3. reeht   _____ interesting

4. aehr   _____ model

5. udnhdres   _____ really

6. eriht   _____ usually

7. uausyll   _____ favorite

8. frefidnet   _____ here

9. riitsp   _____ hear

10. ot   _____ there

11. reeh   _____ their

12. ternitsegni   _____ to

13. eitrovaf   _____ hundreds

14. eallry   _____ tolerance

15. suaeebc   _____ spirit

Modifications

Changes made to student content
and performance expectations.

Alter Expectations

Within a classroom the same activity can be used to
accomplish many different objectives, and can offer different
benefits for different children. It's possible for the entire class
to participate in the same activity, but special and regular
educators are often looking for two very separate objectives.
On appearance it would seem as though there are no
accommodations or modifications being made during some
activities. However, they are being applied subtly behind the
scene. For example, in a reading class the lesson may be on
building reading skills such as main idea, author's purpose,
etc. All students can participate in these activities. It may be
that the regular educator puts emphasis on these activities
because the proficiency deals with many of these reading
skills. Many special education students have reading-oriented
goals on their IEPs that deal with comprehension and
vocabulary. Therefore, the special educator may not want to
put as much graded emphasis on these activities. They still
count. They just don't weigh as much for the student with
special needs as comprehension and vocabulary specific
activities do.

High Points

• Entire class reads the same chapter in a novel.

• Same set of comprehension questions are given to
  all students.

• Regular educator bases grades on complete and thorough
  answers where students specify main idea.

• Special educator bases grades on overall comprehension of
  story, not looking for as many details as the regular
  education teacher is looking for.

• No obvious differences are pointed out.

Context Clues for Vocabulary

Memorizing vocabulary words is a difficult task for many students with special needs. Since some may have a limited vocabulary the class is guided into the discovery of the meaning of these new words by applying context clues. Once the class locates the word in the text, show them how to read around it and 'guess' what they think it means. We have found that this approach works well for both groups of students, as opposed to memorizing dictionary definitions. When vocabulary quizzes are administered, both the special and regular education students receive the same test. While testing, both teachers circulate the room. If a student with special needs is struggling with a word either teacher can put it in context for him, specifically the context in which he was originally introduced to the word. When acceptable to the regular education teacher, the tests can be written in context and given to everyone. Then perhaps the student with special needs would only need a little help with reading content. Either style would be advantageous to struggling students.

High Points

- Direct students to page where vocabulary word is located.

- Use context clues to identify meaning of the word.

- Agree on a definition to be written in notebook.

Modifications are changes made to the content and to each student performance expectation.

- When testing student on vocabulary words, test in context, rather than a memorized dictionary definition. For example: **ignite** – to light or set fire to. At the camp fire, Brian tried to **ignite** the stick.

a.) to break   b.) to light   c.) to shape   d.) to throw

Draw Main Idea

This modification can be used in any subject area, but I will address it in the context of a reading class. As mentioned, comprehension is the biggest difficulty for most struggling students and is one of the primary goals on most IEPs. For example, after reading a designated section of the book, ask students to draw a picture. Then, instruct them to write a few sentences describing their picture to express the main idea it depicts. This activity has been dubbed a 'P & P' – Picture and Paragraph. The regular educator may use this activity as a review for students and for practice in writing

A student drawn main idea that helps visualize reading content.

summary paragraphs. She could therefore grade them accordingly. The special educator, however, may use this activity to measure comprehension. Even though many special education students have trouble answering higher level essay questions, it's still possible to obtain a real understanding of comprehension through their pictures. The paragraph may be weak in grammatical structure but it will convey the degree of comprehension. The special educator may assign a higher point value to this activity than the regular educator. Or the two teachers may assign the same point value, but will remember to look at the activity differently when grading.

Eliminate Higher Level Questions

When studying Bloom's taxonomy of questions, one can see that the acceleration is spread out over a series of steps. It's possible that some struggling students will not move as high up those steps as others. However, this should not be determined before the children are given an opportunity to try. In the coteaching classroom, have all students answer all types of questions. The special educator, upon examining the outcome, may decide not to count the higher level questions in the final assessment. Don't eliminate higher level questions from the student curriculum, just from the grading process when necessary.

High Points

- Have all students attempt all types of questions.
- Based on knowledge of student ability, teacher may or may not count higher level questions such as "how" or "why" type questions.
- As abstract thinking develops, students may begin to master such abstract questions.

Extra Credit for Essay Questions

Often essay questions are included in various assessments. For many students with special needs, especially those with a writing disability, this activity can be almost impossible. As with other modifications, students should be asked to attempt the question. However, if you feel these questions are over the students' heads, don't penalize them for trying it. It can be used as an extra credit question. To encourage students to try their best, it is a good idea to tell them ahead of time what you are planning to do. If the student does a good job in getting the main points across, give them extra credit. If the student is not as successful this time, disregard the question altogether. It's also possible that unthreatening exposure to these questions will lead to more successful answers.

High Points

- Encourage all students to attempt all questions.

- Tell identified students that they won't be penalized for poor answers, just given extra credit for a good answer.

- The same activity/test could have different points for different students.

- Scoring may look like this in your grade book:

Amy	(student with Developmental Disabilities – lacking in general knowledge)	20/24
Sally	(student with Learning Disabilities – poor writing skills)	26/30
Jimmy	(Regular education student – average ability)	35/50

Same test, different points based on individual abilities.

Grade Curving

This is a wonderful modification and can be applied to any content area across the curriculum. As mentioned, all students participate in almost all activities together. This is what helps to spread the 'inclusive feeling' in the coteaching model. However, not everyone is on the same playing field. It's up to you to make the playing field level. That's where this modification comes in. Here's how it works. After a particular test or activity is completed, grade the paper according to standards set previously. Upon completion of grading, separate the papers from students with special needs for calculation purposes. Calculate the mean of the score for both sets of students. The difference between the two means is used as a 'handicap' score to enhance the grades of students with special needs. This is not spelled out to the student and a letter grade is all that appears on the child's paper. Extra points are included before the letter grade is given. Also, the extra points are noted in the grade book. This is another 'behind the scene' modification that insures fairness within the classroom.

Regular Education Student Scores	Special Education Student Scores
43/50	37/50
38/50	40/50
47/50	33/50
49/50	28/50
45/50	35/50
Mean = 44/50	35/50

** An additional 9 points is added to each of the special education students score as a "handicap" to level the playing field.

Your grade book may look something like this after you have recorded the scores:

Student				Final Score
Amy L.	37	9		46
Sally S.	40	9		49
Jimmy D.	33	9		42
Billy M.	28	9		37
Bobby F.	35	9		44
Total Points	**50**	**0**		**50**

** It's important that the special educator be responsible for the grading of her students. Generally these modifications and accommodations are discussed among the teaching team and mutually agreed upon. But, the ultimate responsibility of grading the students with special needs is with their teacher.

Guided Worksheets

This modification saves a great deal of frustration on the part of student and teacher. When the class is responding to short answer or essay questions at the end of a chapter, searching for it among 10 – 15 pages often feels like looking for a needle in a haystack for struggling students. Not only do they struggle with reading, but also with reading strategies, like skimming a chapter. Therefore, when the special educator gives these types of activities, it's helpful if she writes a page number beside the question on which the answer can be found. Once the student gets to that page, the student with special needs can demonstrate how to skim that page, or the column, to find the answer. The student is doing the same work, once again, just performing it within tighter boundaries.

Chapter 5, Lesson 1

Guided Questions

1. What helped make the Fertile Crescent fertile? (p. 104)
2. What is a plateau? (p. 105)
3. How did Mesopotamia's floods benefit farmers there? (p. 105)
4. How did floods bring misfortune? (p. 105)
5. How did they regulate the amount of water flowing into the canals? (p. 106)
6. How did Mesopotamia get its name? (p. 107)
7. What did the Tigris and the Euphrates provide for Mesopotamia? (p. 107)

Individual Expectations

This is similar to the modification addressing altered expectations. When a student with special needs is participating in an activity like writing, the teacher can individualize student expectations based on the goals of his IEP. The assignment may be to compile a three-paragraph essay following the structure of an introductory sentence, with details and a conclusion. However, maybe one or more of the students with special needs are working on writing a complete sentence. Therefore, when the child's paper is being graded, that is what the teacher is focusing in on. Maybe another student with special needs has mastered sentence writing and is working on writing one successful paragraph. This is what the teacher should focus on when grading his paper. Individual, quick meetings can be held with the students in class to help foster their personal goals in writing. In general, the creative writing assignment appears identical throughout the entire class, but the level of expectation is significantly different based on the goals stated in student IEPs.

High Points

- Individual Expectations.

- All students follow same directions for same writing piece.

- IEP student is working on completing a complete sentence, and demonstrating knowledge of a paragraph.

- Regular education students are working on properly structuring a three paragraph essay.

- During grading process, special education teacher and regular education teacher are looking for individual expectations.

- Both teachers grade accordingly.

Mastery Learning

As teachers, our main objective is to help all children become the best possible person they can become. For every student this means something different, and is accomplished in different time spans. After all, we didn't all learn to walk at the exact same time, but eventually we all got the hang of it. That same philosophy holds true for learning anything. Some of our students are not ready to successfully take a test or perform a given activity at the time we have deemed appropriate. Why cut off their learning after the first attempt? If a student is willing to continue trying, I for one would never say no to that. It's strongly recommended that children not only be permitted but encouraged to correct their work in any subject area. Full credit should then be given for this corrected work. If the child is willing to go back and study harder for a test or re-work the problems in math they have achieved the objective of the lesson and should be graded accordingly.

High Points

- As teachers, our main objective is to help students learn.

- Allow students to correct their work, as often as necessary.

- Give full credit for corrected work.

- Practice makes perfect!

Your grade book may look like this:

Student	Act. 1	Act. 2	Act. 3	Act. 4	Act. 5
Amy	~~15~~ 25	15	35	~~10~~ 13	~~6~~ 9
Sally	~~27~~ 30	~~10~~ 13	~~27~~ 30	15	8
Susan	20	~~9~~ 12	~~25~~ 35	~~10~~ 15	~~7~~ 9
Billy	~~10~~ 25	13	30	18	~~4~~ 6
Jimmy	~~25~~ 27	10	~~15~~ 25	~~12~~ 17	~~5~~ 8
Total Points	30	15	40	20	10

Provide Starter Sentences

Communication, especially written, is difficult for many of our students with special needs. Sometimes, they just need a little spark to get the fire started. This modification can be used anywhere writing is taking place. The teachers can privately provide the student with a few starter sentences to get a writing piece going. Or she can provide a few key phrases to get an idea onto the paper. This does not mean to suggest that 'giving answers' is appropriate at any time. However, laying out a few clues, and watching the students faces respond with "Oh, yeah," is just helping to get things started.

High Points

- Class is given a writing assignment on a particular topic.

- Student with special needs has no idea where to begin.

- Special education teacher brainstorms with student sub-topics about which student can write.

- Together they choose one topic, teacher provides a starting sentence or a few key phrases to get the student engaged in writing.

- Once student is on her way, she is left to complete writing piece individually.

Read and Explain Tests

This modification can be used in any area but I'm going to refer to Social Studies and Science. When a test is being administered, it's not always necessary that struggling students receive a different test. Remember, modifications and accommodations should be administered in a sensitive, subtle manner. So, students can usually use the same test. Split the class by having the special educator offer to read the test to anyone who wants it read. This is done after the class has learned about "different learning modalities" and students are exposed to discovering their favored one. The student with special needs goes with the teacher to a different classroom to take their test. Of course, this should be varied once in a while by having the regular education students leave when children with special needs stay in the classroom. Once testing has started, the special educator can read the test to the class. After reading each question, explain it to the class. Often when we are assessing students, we get an inaccurate picture of their knowledge because they either can't read the question or don't know what the question is asking. Be sure this obstacle is eliminated.

Also, before the testing begins, it's often necessary to eliminate test anxiety from many of our struggling students. Tell the class you are going to read and explain the test to them. Instruct them to answer as many questions as they are sure of. At the end of the testing period, allow them to use notes to look up anything they are unsure of. Make them aware that it has to be their notes they are referring to and not the text book. Once the test is read and explained, give them the time you promised with their notes.

In Social Studies and Science many abstract concepts are taught. This type of thinking is difficult for many struggling students to comprehend. By allowing them to use their notes we are saying that we know it is difficult to remember all this information, but what you cannot remember you must write down so you're able to access when necessary. This is a skill that can be implemented into everyday life. This modification has proven to be very successful.

High Points

- Teacher says to class, "anyone who wants the test read to them, come with me."

- Class is then split into two groups – those who want the test read to them and those who want to read the test alone.

Note: Most students with special needs will go with the group that wants the test read to them.

- Not only does the teacher read the test, she also explains what each question is asking. At this time she may eliminate one of the multiple choice answers to narrow it down to three possible answers.

- Before testing begins, eliminate anxiety by telling the class that they may use their notes during the last ten minutes or so of the testing period.

- If the whole test was not covered in this time period, only hold students accountable for the part of the test you were able to read to them.

Re-Test Orally

Often, auditory learners are also auditory testers. A child with a severe writing disability may be knowledgeable in the content area but unable to give it back to the teacher for assessment purposes in a written format. Of course, as teachers we want to work on improving the student's writing ability. Therefore, with this modification the student takes the written test with the rest of the group. As the teacher, you have an idea about who understands what. If the score on the written test is contrary to what you feel may be true of the student, allow him to retest with you privately in an oral format. This way you are really assessing knowledge content and not just writing ability.

High Points

• Due to poor written communication skills, child tests poorly on written test.

• After having attempted the written test, ask child to re-test orally.

• Grade student on knowledge of content, not ability to correctly communicate knowledge in writing.

Set Up Calculation for Word Problems on Daily Work and Tests

Obviously this modification is applicable to math only. As was mentioned before, it is good practice to have the struggling students use the same book, keep the same pace, and work on the exact same curriculum as the rest of the class whenever possible. Of course, this is not always possible but for social acceptance this is the optimum situation. However, math in the upper grades is often heavily concentrated with word problems and they are difficult for many students with special needs. Therefore, the special educator can develop a worksheet that bridges the gap for this student's thinking. Instruct the student to read the word problem in the book. Then have the students refer to the worksheet made by the teacher. The worksheet should have the word problem set up for calculation. The child then completes the calculation. This modification should be delivered for all word problems initially. As the student is exposed to the same type problem over and over again, begin a weaning process by gradually pulling concepts away as they have been reinforced sufficiently throughout the program. Remember, this is not intended to be a tool used permanently. Ideally, after having modeled for the student several times how to go about transferring a specific word problem into a calculation problem, eventually the student will be able to do this on his own. This can be done with daily work as well as tests.

The following is an example of a group of problems that could be found in any Middle School math book and a worksheet I have made to coincide with these problems. From the first day of school, the students are instructed to use these worksheets along with the book or test. Used in isolation they would serve no purpose. This concept is later reinforced with the parents at our open house.

All of the sixth grade classes in our school use the same math book, including the inclusion class. As you can see, many of these are word problems that can cause difficulty for a child who has learning disabilities in reading or writing. It's important to mention that we offer these "worksheets" to any student who wants them. Initially, many regular education students ask for them. Eventually though, given the tedious nature of going through the problem, many typical students find these worksheets too time consuming and opt not to use them. It's at this time that my partner teacher and I go into a little explanation of how everyone learns differently and we need to find which way works best for us.

Name_____ Date _____ Daily Work _____

1) 5 2/8 + 7 5/8 =

2) There are 100 centimeters in a meter. There are 1,000 meters in a kilometer. How many centimeters are in a kilometer?

3) One eighth of a circle is 12 1/2% of a circle. What percent of a circle is 3/8 of a circle?

4) What is the greatest common factor of 15 and 25?

5) Write 1 and 4/5 as a mixed number.

6) Jimmy rode his skate board to the mall and back. If the trip was 5 3/4 miles each way, how far did he ride in all?

7) What is the **eighth** number in this sequence? 8, 16, 24, 32, 40, . . .

8) Add and simplify: 3/5 + 4/5 =

9) What is the least common multiple of both 12 and 18?

10) Compare: _ plus _ _ of _

11) 2/3 + <u>N</u> = 1

12) The young alligator was 36 months old. How many years old was this alligator?

13) Write a fraction that is equal to one that has a denominator of eight.

14) What is the perimeter of an equilateral triangle with sides measuring 2/3?

15) Eileen bought 3 _ dozen chocolate chip cookies to school for a party. This was enough for how many children to have one cookie each?

Practical Strategies for Middle School Inclusion

Name _____ Date _____ Daily Work _____

1) $5\frac{2}{8} + 7\frac{5}{8} =$ a. Add numerator $2 + 5 =$ __ b. Put numerator over 8 c. Add $5 + 7 =$ __ $\frac{\underline{\quad}}{8}$	2) 100 cm = 1 m 1000 m = k $\quad$ 1000 m X 100 cm $\quad$ K	3) $\frac{1}{8} = 12\ 1/2\%$ $\frac{3}{8} = 3 \times 12\ 1/2\%$ $\frac{3}{1} \times \frac{25}{2} =$
4) $15 =$ __, __, __, __ $25 =$ __, __, __	5) 1 4/5 as mixed number. $5 \times 1 + 4 = 9$ $\frac{9}{5}$ $5\ \overline{)\ 9}$	6) $5\frac{3}{4} \times 2 = (4 \times 5 + 3)$ $\frac{23}{4} \times \frac{2}{1} =$
7) 8, 16, 24, 32, 40, __, __, __ Increasing by how much? 8th Number = ____	8) $\frac{3}{5} + \frac{4}{5} = \dfrac{\quad}{5}$ $5\ \overline{\quad}$	9) $12=$ __, __, __, __ $\quad$ 12x1 12x2 12x3 12x4 $18=$ __, __, __, __ $\quad$ 18x1 18x2 18x3 18x4
10) $\frac{1}{2} + \frac{1}{2} = (a)$ ____ Remember "of" means x's $\frac{1}{2} \times \frac{1}{2} = (b)$ ____ (a) ____ > or < (b) ____	11) $\frac{2}{3} + N = 1$ Remember 1 could = $^3/_3$ $\frac{2}{3} + N = \frac{3}{3}$ $N =$ ____	12) Remember there are 12 months in one year. $12\overline{)\ 36\ months}^{\ years}$
13) Remember, the fraction line means division. $\frac{\underline{\quad}}{8} = 1$ What # divided by 8 = 1?	14) Perimeter = all 3 sides. Equilateral means equal sides. $\frac{2}{3} + \frac{2}{3} + \frac{2}{3} = \overline{3}$ $3\ \overline{\quad}$	15) Remember, a dozen = 12 $3\_ = (3 \times 12) + (^1/_2\ of\ 12)$ ____ + ____ = ____

Test

Name _____

1) Round 75,248 to the nearest thousand.

2) What is the reciprocal of $\frac{1}{3}$?

3) What is the perimeter of a square which has sides 6 inches long?

4) What is the area of a room that measures 8 ft. by 12 ft.?

5) Which digit in 5.234 is in the hundredths' place?

6) Write the decimal numeral twelve thousandths.

7) Write (5 x 100) + (6 x 1) in standard notation.

8) Two days is what fraction of a week?

9) Write 0.47 as a common fraction.

10) Compare: $\frac{3}{4}$ $\frac{4}{3}$

Name _____ Date _____ Daily Work _____

1) 75,284 = __ __, __ __ __	2) Remember, reciprocal means to flip. Reciprocal of $\frac{1}{3}$ =
3) Perimeter of a square. Square has 4 equal sides. Each side is 6 inches long. Add all the sides. Perimeter = _____	4) Area = Length x Width Area = _____ x _____ Area = _____
5) 5.234 Hundredths place is _____ Remember: hundred**ths** is **after** the decimal. (The "th" tells us that)	6) . __ __ __
7) 5 x 100 = _____ 6 x 1 = _____ + _____	8) 2 days out of 7 days. Write as a fraction. The part on top and the whole on bottom.
9) 0.47 as a fraction. <u>47</u>	10) $\frac{3}{4}$ > or < $\frac{4}{3}$

Structure Tests

This modification can be used to compliment the previous one that reads and explains tests to struggling students. It's not always necessary to administer a different test to students with special needs, though this decision needs to be made on a case by case basis. However, many struggling students can take the exact same test as the regular education students with subtle modifications in place. Remember, these tests may be hanging in the classroom and the more sensitive you are to student individual needs, the better. In addition to reading and explaining the test to them, some still need a little more structure. Generally in the content subjects, tests are made up of matching tests, multiple choice, fill in the blank and essay questions. We have already discussed how teachers can handle essay questions. For the matching test portion, be sure that the word and its match appear on the same page, if it is a multiple page test. For the multiple choice portion the special needs' teacher could tell the students, while she is reading the test, one or even two of the choices that are incorrect. In most multiple choice tests there are generally two answers that are obviously wrong and two that could very well be correct. Eliminate one of the close answers, leaving the correct and the (two obviously) incorrect answers to choose from. In doing so, you are teaching your students test taking skills. For the fill-in-the blank portion of the test, on a separate piece of paper, provide a word bank for the students to refer to. This bank can be discarded after the test. Often the written disability gets in the way of the student conveying to the teacher the knowledge that he does have. Providing the word bank eliminates anxiety over spelling or difficulty recalling abstract terms.

Often the special educator will read and explain the tests to her students. It's possible that in doing so, the test will not be completed in the time period allotted. The teacher then needs to make a decision in consultation with her coteacher. Maybe there is a study hall or another time period when she can work with her students to complete the test. If not, then the struggling students can be graded on the portion they are able to complete. It's better for the student to do part of an activity, and do it well, than complete it with poor quality. Remember to stay as close to the objective as possible in everything you do with your students. If you are assessing knowledge, assess a small piece at a time and reward students for mastering it, rather than demanding all the information be assessed and eliminating even small successes from students. At all times try to set students up to be successful!

High Points

- Read and explain tests to students.
- Essay questions regarded as extra credit.
- Matching test – have the word and its match appear on the same page.
- Multiple choice portion – teacher can give students one or two choices to eliminate, leaving just two or three to choose from.
- Provide word banks for fill-in-the-blank questions. Make sure the word bank is a perfect match to the fill-in questions. If necessary, print the word bank on a separate sheet of paper and discard after testing.
- Grade only the completed portion of the test.
- Don't penalize student for working at a slower pace.

Teacher and Student Create Outline

When a student has a learning disability or limited general knowledge it's often difficult for them to progress on their own from a blank piece of paper to completion without guidance to get started. This can be used in writing activities of any kind. The teacher simply brainstorms aloud with the student and finds out what he knows and what he wants to write about. From there the teacher models for them how to create an outline, helping take his thoughts from his head to paper in an organized fashion. Modeling may need to be done just one or two times with some students before they are able to perform this task on their own, while with others it may need to be done numerous times. It will take different techniques for different students. For some students this modification is best used with the Starter Sentence modification, but for others that's not necessary. Get to know the students and give them as many tools as they need to be successful in the classroom. Remember, some students have never been in a large classroom before. Just sitting in a room with 25 to 30 other students makes them nervous. Study your students beyond their IEP goals and do whatever it takes to help them build self esteem by showing them that they can be successful if they try.

High Points

- Writing activity is assigned to class.

- Teacher and student set up a web or an outline easy for the student to follow.

- Could provide starter sentences as well.

- Work with the student until she is at a safe place to be left to her own writing without suffering anxiety feelings due to inadequacies.

Use Notes During Test

This modification is to be used in conjunction with the Skeletal Set of Notes Accommodation. Here, the education teacher provides the class with notes. Students who have difficulty writing are provided with a skeletal set of notes which are stapled into their notebook and studied in preparation for the test. Instruct the students to have their notes on the day of the test. It's important to pay close attention to the way you word things when you are talking to the struggling student. You never want to project the message that they are less able than a typical student. Be sensitive and fair at the same time and chose your words wisely. Once the groups have been separated for testing, tell the struggling

It's important to pay close attention to the way you word things when you are talking to the struggling student. You never want to project the message that they are less able than a typical student.

students they are to complete as much of the test as they can. For questions that students didn't immediately recall, give them a brief opportunity at the end of the testing period to use their notes. I have found that 10 to 13 minutes is enough time. You don't want this to be a situation where the student is copying information from one piece of paper to another. This is only a small modification. Assessment is still the objective here. The key word is 'their notes.' If they don't know where their notes are, or they didn't complete them due to poor choices on their part, then they are out of luck. With this modification, conscientious students are rewarded for their effort. Taking good notes, studying them and trying your best is all any teacher can ask of her students. When you know the limited abilities of some, this resource makes the playing field a little more level. At the same time we are teaching students a life skill. Many adults cannot remember all the information they need to complete their numerous tasks throughout the day, but they certainly know how to find it out when it's needed.

High Points

- Separate class for testing as discussed earlier.

- Encourage students to complete as much of the test as they can on immediate recall.

- Tell students they will be given time at the end of the testing period to look up anything they were unsure of. This helps to eliminate test anxiety.

- Direct the student to use only their notes: They must be organized and available.

- This teaches students that if they are unable to recall information by memory, it's necessary for them to be organized enough to know where to find that information when necessary.

Individual/Small Group Tutoring

Even with all these modifications in place, a child will need to correct a paper, have a concept re-explained to him, make up missed work, study for a test, or need help getting through homework. It's recommended that the special education teacher plan into her day a time when she can perform these tasks with her students. It's not always possible to do this during the school day, so an alternative is to schedule before or after school. Whenever this can be arranged, it's very advantageous to the struggling student.

Due to the fact that sometimes there are more students in need of help than one teacher can possibly get to, it's suggested that a peer tutoring program be set up to assist struggling students. Many higher level students can serve as very successful tutors for students in need. Studies show that peers learn well with other students. This is different from pairing high with low students in the classroom. In that setting the higher level student has a stake in the outcome and can feel frustrated in the situation. In a tutoring setting, it's clear from the beginning who is the tutor and who is being tutored.

Due to the fact that sometimes there are more students in need of help than one teacher can possibly get to, it's suggested that a peer tutoring program be set up to assist struggling students.

Conclusion

Decisions should be made by team teachers in a cooperative environment. Parents should be made aware of strategies being implemented and may assist you in determining other strategies that may also be helpful. The IEP team is only successful when the child is successful.

The accommodations and modifications outlined in this manual are just some suggestions of how to assist students in the classroom. It's not intended to exclude other strategies. Some identified students will need all of these strategies whereas others may only need a few. Many of these strategies are used in conjunction with each other. Determinating which to use is based on the unique individual needs of the child. These decisions should be made by team teachers in a cooperative environment. Parents should be made aware of strategies being implemented and can assist you in determining other strategies that may also be helpful. The IEP team is only successful when the child is successful.

Due to their disabilities, these modifications and accommodations are given to struggling students in order for them to be successful in the regular education classroom. If teachers are modifying a student's curriculum on a daily basis, it would be unreasonable of us to expect that child to pass something like our Ohio Proficiency Test without similar modifications. As teachers we are held accountable for these modifications. Since they are impossible to implement during the proficiency test, it's reasonable to exempt these student from the test. If they have been exposed to the regular education curriculum in an inclusive classroom, have them take the test. However, if they can't be successful in the classroom without these modifications it's unfair to expect them to succeed without them on a proficiency test.

The coteaching model is one more service available on a continuum. Remember that inclusion is not for every student. Every child must be considered individually on a case-by-case situation. It's up to the IEP team to determine the least restrictive environment for that individual child. The inclusion program is a least restrictive option, but some children may need more restriction. The IEP team must make educated decisions concerning this child's best placement on the continuum of services.

5

How Do I Organize All This?

Academic Snapshot and Educational Prescriptions

Two of the biggest complaints in special education are the lack of documentation and of objectivity used in decision making. Administrators, parents and others are beginning to ask, "where is the data?" "Show me the evidence that brought you to this decision." It's understandable that special educators are somewhat subjective because we are trained to find individual differences in children and work around them. However, there is room to improve and learning how to document more thoroughly and in a more objective fashion would help us assist children more efficiently.

In an effort to accomplish these two goals, I have developed two forms to be used with each student, the Academic Snapshot and the Educational Prescription.

The first form to discuss is the Academic Snapshot. It has several useful purposes.

Academic Snapshot

The IEPs most states use are becoming more detailed all the time. Although this information is necessary, it's sometimes easier to have more basic data at your fingertips, that is, a "snapshot." The Academic Snapshot provides you with valuable information at a glance.

The second purpose it has is to provide the IEP team with each student's starting point each year, providing you with objective, measurable growth. Often times the receiving teacher will find this information on the IEP. My personal preference, however, is to obtain this information myself when the student comes to me in September. This form should be used to record student levels of academic functioning in reading, writing and math skills. This information is then documented on the Academic Snapshot in the beginning of the school year and again towards the end. Used in this manner, a teacher can objectively measure and illustrate growth that is clear and easy to see.

I have found the revised version of the Brigance Test of Basic Skills to be a user friendly tool in assessing these areas. The test is diagnostic in nature, lending itself to a specific breakdown of information outlining skills that the student has or has not mastered. The special education teacher can use this test in the early part of the school year, record the results on the Academic Snapshot and work from there. This pre-test gives the teacher the baseline data necessary to begin instruction. As the year draws to a close, the special educator administers this test again and records the results on the Academic Snapshot. She now has a beginning and an ending point with which she can measure growth. This test has 2 forms which accommodate pre-and-post-test teaching. If all teachers dealing with the same children were using the same test, it would be even more valid. This consistency would allow for a fair and even measure of growth.

Next, the form shows professionals the learning modalities and discrepancies of each student. From there it is easy to develop accommodations and modifications that help fill in gaps for weak areas of struggling students. Then an individual curriculum can be developed. Once the Academic Snapshot is completed, the Educational Prescription becomes an easy fix. For example, if the student is entering the sixth grade and is proven to be functioning on a fourth grade silent reading comprehension level but a sixth grade listening comprehension level, then it's advantageous for the teacher to provide him with as much oral reading opportunities as possible. This could be accomplished by having the teacher or another student read it to him, providing him with a book on tape, etc. At the same time, you could encourage him to follow along while listening to the reading in an effort to help build his sight vocabulary. By implementing this strategy, you allow the student an opportunity to comprehend the material by channeling it through his strong learning modality and at the same time to strengthen his weak modality.

Finally, when it is complete, it's easy to see where the child is functioning, and what his strengths and weaknesses are. It's reasonable to assume that if a student is functioning two or more years below grade level, he will have difficulty working within the general curriculum even with lengthy modifications. This gives the IEP team the objective data needed to make an educated decision on the best possible placement for this child. Depending on where he is functioning, maybe an inclusion classroom on a grade level or two below would be a good placement option, or possibly a resource room. The options are as varied as the team is creative. This Academic Snapshot gives the team the information needed to make this reliable decision.

Academic Snapshot

_____   _____
Name   Date

READING				
Sil. Read. Comp.	Listen. Comp.	Vocab. Comp.	Oral Read (text)	Oral Read (list)

MATH				
Grade Level	Word Problem	Whole # Comp.	Decimal Comp.	Fraction Comp.

ENGLISH		
Spelling Level	Sentence Writing Level	Paragraph Writing

PROFICIENCY		
Exempt/Not Exempt	Areas Not Tested	Modifications

Other Information _____

_____

_____

The Educational Prescription

As a sixth grade special educator it has always amazed me that our students have existed within the school district for as long as five years or more prior to entering Middle School and teachers prior to me have figured out how they learn best and what they can and can't do within the general curriculum. Unfortunately, they have no easy means of sharing this information with the receiving teacher. Hence, the Educational Prescription. Rather than force each teacher every year to take five to six weeks to figure out how best to work with this child, why not pass recommended accommodations and modifications on from year to year? That's where the form title comes from; it's a description of a learning prescription that has proven successful for this student in the past. When the receiving teacher gets this student, she will receive the IEP along with the Educational Prescription.

Those who know our students the best are their parents. Each special educator should speak with the parent of each student in the beginning of the year. At that time, ask them for information about their child that helps you assist her better. For example, maybe they will tell you their daughter is not a very good writer, but loves to listen to people read or tell stories to her. This tells you that her auditory skills are strong. Possibly, in addition to oral reading, you could assist the student and her parents with putting her spelling or vocabulary words on tape so she could access her strong learning channel to learn necessary curriculum. Our parents are our best source of information for our students. They were their child's first teacher, and have watched her grow and develop. They know what has worked well in the past and what has not. Tap into this source of information and document that information on the Educational Prescription.

This form also serves as a form of documentation to justify, or explain, decisions. For example, some states have statewide proficiency tests that are administered over a series of varied grades. In some states, student school diplomas hinge on the success rate of this test. In addition, most states are encouraging teachers to have special education students take these tests. And in many cases, special education students have proven to be successful with this assessment. However, some states have left room for them to take these tests but allow them to be exempt from the accountably of passing if they have been receiving considerable modifications to their daily curriculum. Remember, a modification is a significant change made to the curriculum, and different from an accommodation. When viewing the Educational Prescription, if there are only a few modifications suggested, the child may not need to be exempt. If, however, their curriculum contains many modifications, holding them accountable for this test without offering the same modifications would not be reasonable. The Educational Prescription is a tool that demonstrates what modifications are being administered and to what degree they are being delivered.

Educational Prescription

Present Levels of Performance	Sub/Act	Goal	Objective	Accommodations

Student _____ Parents _____ Date/Grade _____ Phone # _____

Status	Modifications	Status	Areas of Concern	Points of Interest	Consultation

How Do I Organize All This Information?

Next I will take you through the paper trail of one student, Jimmy Smith (not his name). The information pertaining to this student has not been changed in any way.

The first step to the process is to use an assessment tool. I prefer the Brigance Test of Basic Skills, to complete the **Academic Snapshot** in September. Once this is completed, you can fill in the **Educational Prescription**. Admittedly, it is lengthy, but after you have completed it in September, it doesn't have to be done again. This form becomes your guide to assist in helping the child surmount his learning disabilities. These strategies help him progress from where he is presently functioning to grade level, or close to it. You will refer to this form often throughout the year. At times you may feel it is necessary to discontinue a strategy. That can be inserted in the "status" column. This form is a wealth of information and can be shared with his teachers that follow you.

After the Educational Prescription you will find a two-page explanation of the accommodations and modifications I selected. This should help you in analyzing data on individual students.

Next you will find a second copy of the September Academic Snapshot followed immediately by the Snapshot taken in March. This will assist you in seeing a "before and after" picture of the student's accomplishments in sixth grade.

And finally, I have inserted a copy of the first page of this student's IEP. As you can see, these present levels of performance are recorded directly from the March Snapshot.

It's impossible to "standardize" this procedure. My intention here is to show you how to create this paper trail. Due to the individual nature of our business, this procedure can only be customized to fit the needs of individual students.

Lastly, I have included a blank copy of the Academic Snapshot and the Educational Prescription. Feel free to copy and use these in your classroom.

Academic Snapshot

<u>Jimmy Smith (L.D.)</u>   <u>Sept, 2003</u>
Name   Date

READING				
Sil. Read. Comp.	Listen. Comp.	Vocab. Comp.	Oral Read (text)	Oral Read (list)
Mastered 4th Functioning 5th	Mastered 5th w/100% Functioning 6th	Mastered 3rd Functioning 4th Gr.		

MATH				
Grade Level	Word Problem	Whole # Comp.	Decimal Comp.	Fraction Comp.
Mastered 4th Gr. Functioning 5th Gr.	Mastered 5th Gr. Functioning 6th Gr.	Had difficulty w/3D X3D & Long division	Could not +, -, x, ÷ Decimals	Could not +, -, x, ÷ Fractions

ENGLISH		
Spelling Level	Sentence Writing Level	Paragraph Writing
Mastered 4th Gr. Functioning 5th Gr.	Mastered 4th Gr. Functioning 5th Gr.	No Reference made in IEP.

PROFICIENCY		
Exempt/Not Exempt	Areas Not Tested	Modifications
All area's tested		

Other Information _____

_____

_____

Educational Prescription

Present Levels of Performance	Sub/Act	Goal	Objective	Accommodations
Silent Reading – functioning 5th grade Listening Comprehension – functioning 6th grade Vocabulary Comprehension – functioning 4th grade	Reading	Demonstrate comprehension of classroom material.	- inferring, details, main idea and cause/effect - reading vocab. - participate in class answering questions.	- Cooperative Learning - Oral Reading
Grade Level – functioning 5th Word Problem – functioning 6th Could not -X 3D 3D. -do long div., no skill w/ fractions or Decimals.	Math	None stated on IEP		- Correct mistakes w/ calculator. Initially try w/o calculator.
Spelling Level - functioning 5th grade Sentence Writing – functioning 5th grade.	English	- to complete classroom writing assignments.	- write neatly w/correct spelling, punc., grammar. - write para. - pass spelling tests	- Written spelling tests - color code spelling words - words on tape
- Inability or unwillingness to complete assignments. - Receives failing grades for incomplete work.	Vocational	Demonstrate strategies for completing all assignments.	- use an assignment book - stay organized w/folders	- assignment initial program - home school communication - locker organization
	Social studies and Science			- develop study guide - skeletal set of notes - vocabulary words on tape

Student _____ Parents _____ Date/Grade _____ Phone # _____

Status	Modifications	Status	Areas of Concern	Points of Interest	Consultation
	- Alter expectations - Context clues for vocabulary - Draw main idea		- Weak phonic decoding skills - Overwhelmed by large amounts of print	- Likes cars & racing - Likes to draw	- IEP - Mom
	- Calculation sheets (wean off slowly) - Mastery learning		- Doesn't know multiplication facts - Refuses to complete homework		- Mom -Mom
	- Provide starter sentence - Teacher/student create outline - Alter expectations		- Writing well below grade level -Poor spelling, word usage, capitalization - Writes simple short sentences routinely		- IEP - IEP - IEP
			- Difficulty completing work - Communication skills average - Developing attitude/behaviors that are interfering w/school		- IEP & Mom - IEP - IEP & Mom
	- Guided worksheets - Read & explain tests _ Structure tests - Context clues for vocabulary - Use notes during tests				

Why Choose These Specific Accommodations/Modifications for Jimmy Smith?

Reading

Cooperative Learning – adds a "social" component to reading.

Oral Reading – Jimmy's listening comprehension is stronger than his silent reading comprehension.

Alter Expectations – initially Jimmy needs to experience success. Expectations can be raised once Jimmy believes he can do the work successfully.

Context Clues for Vocabulary – Jimmy's vocabulary comprehension is far below grade level. Memorizing words is not working for him. Putting words in context may assist in understanding meaning.

Draw Main Idea – to strengthen the silent reading level, Jimmy needs to be taught how to "draw" the story in his minds eye. This strategy may help.

Math

Calculation Sheets – Jimmy had been refusing to complete homework. These sheets may make the work more manageable. Wean off as time goes by.

Mastery Learning – This will assist Jimmy is learning from his mistakes. It also demonstrates to him that his success is important to his teacher, as well as to himself.

English

Written Spelling Tests – Jimmy needs to be able to identify the correct spelling of a word. Visually memorizing how to spell words has not worked for Jimmy in the past.

Color Code Spelling Words – Jimmy's visual skills are not that weak. This strategy may work.

Words on Tape – Jimmy's auditory skills are stronger than his visual skills as demonstrated in his reading comprehension. "Hearing" the spelling of the word may assist Jimmy in mastering his list of words.

Provide Starter Sentences – Jimmy is not an ambitious student. He needs help getting started on a project. Offering initial assistance increases the possibility that he may complete the assignment.

Teacher/student create outline – this skill teaches Jimmy how to begin and organize a paragraph.

Vocational

Assignment Initial Program – Jimmy needs to see that he is being held accountable for the completion of his assignments both by his parents and by his teacher. Not completing his work has been a serious problem of Jimmy's in the past.

Home School Communication – Jimmy's Mom was very much willing to get involved in Jimmy's school work. Help at home can only enhance Jimmy's chances for success.

Locker Organization – Jimmy had difficulty staying organized in elementary school as evidenced by his teachers comments on his IEP. This problem can only compound itself in Middle School. Teaching Jimmy organizational skills is mandatory.

Social Studies and Science

Develop Study Guides – Jimmy's lack of organizational skills contributes to his inability to organized his study material. Study guides provide direction.

Skeletal Set of Notes – Jimmy's fifth grade teacher expressed concern about Jimmy completing classroom work, and writing neatly. Copying a complete set of notes off the board may not be accomplished completely and/or accurately.

Vocabulary Words on Tape – This strategy takes advantage of Jimmy's strong auditory skills.

Guided Worksheets – Jimmy's Mom expressed concern that Jimmy is overwhelmed by large amounts of print. He will have difficulty searching 10 pages for the answer to an essay question.

Read and Explain Tests – Along with study skills, Jimmy needs to learn test taking strategies. This strategy could aid in that development.

Structure Tests – Jimmy's lack of success in the classroom has created anxiety and self doubt in his own ability. These ideas need to be eliminated from Jimmy's mind. Structured tests will mostly likely bring success.

Use Notes During Tests – Jimmy has illustrated a weakness in memorizing by demonstrating poor spelling and vocabulary ability. He may never be able to memorize all the needed material for a test. We need to teach him how to work around this deficit.

Academic Snapshot

Jimmy Smith (L.D.)   Sept, 2003

Name   Date

READING				
Sil. Read. Comp.	Listen. Comp.	Vocab. Comp.	Oral Read (text)	Oral Read (list)
Mastered 4th Functioning 5th	Mastered 5th w/100% Functioning 6th	Mastered 3rd Functioning 4th Gr.		

MATH				
Grade Level	Word Problem	Whole # Comp.	Decimal Comp.	Fraction Comp.
Mastered 4th Gr. Functioning 5th Gr.	Mastered 5th Gr. Functioning 6th Gr.	Had difficulty w/3D X3D & long division	Could not +, -, x, ÷ Decimals	Could not +, -, x, ÷ Fractions

ENGLISH		
Spelling Level	Sentence Writing Level	Paragraph Writing
Mastered 4th Gr. Functioning 5th Gr.	Mastered 4th Gr. Functioning 5th Gr.	No Reference made in IEP.

PROFICIENCY		
Exempt/Not Exempt	Areas Not Tested	Modifications
All area's tested		

Other Information _____

_____

_____

Academic Snapshot

Jimmy Smith (L.D.)   March 26, 2004
Name   Date

READING				
Sil. Read. Comp.	Listen. Comp.	Vocab. Comp.	Oral Read (text)	Oral Read (list)
Mastered 7th w/80% Functioning 8th Gr.	Mastered 7th Gr. Functioning 8th w/60%	Mastered 5th Gr. Functioning 6th Gr.	Mastered 6th (2 errors) Functioning 7th (5 errors)	

MATH				
Grade Level	Word Problem	Whole # Comp.	Decimal Comp.	Fraction Comp.
Mastered 5th Gr. Functioning 6th Gr. *	On grade level.	75% w/o calculator, 100% w/calculator. Had problems dividing	4 operations 100% w/calculator, 66% w/o calculator.	Could + - x like/unlike fractions. Difficulty w/÷ fractions.

Understands division concept.

ENGLISH		
Spelling Level	Sentence Writing Level	Paragraph Writing
Mastered 5th Gr. Functioning 6th Gr.	On grade level.	Understands what constitutes a paragraph.

PROFICIENCY		
Exempt/Not Exempt	Areas Not Tested	Modifications
Passed all 5 area's of the 6th grade proficiency test.		Tested in a small group. Tests read to him, except reading test.

Other Information _____

*He had difficulty adding unlike fractions, difficulty multiplying fractions w/mixed numbers & difficulty dividing decimals.

☐ **Service Plan**   **Willoughby-Eastlake City Schools**   **Individualized Education Program (IEP)**

Name _____   Date of Birth _____   Grade Level _____   ☒ Male ☐ Female

Student identification Number _____

Child/Student Address _____

Parent Address _____   Parent/Guardian _____

_____   Home phone _____   Work Phone _____

Effective Dates from _8/28/2002_ to _6/6/2003_   Meeting Date _____   ☐ Initial IEP ☒ Periodic Review

District of Residence _____   District of Service _Willoughby-Eastlake School District_

Step 1: Discuss Vision: Future Planning

Step 2: Discuss Present Levels of Performance

has done a great job this year. His successful growth and development has been a joy to watch. His silent reading level comprehension has grown leaps and bounds this year. In September he was functioning on a 5th grade silent reading level and when tested in March with the same Brigance Test of Basic skills. proved to be at or very close to grade level in his silent reading comprehension. He has progressed a year in his listening comprehension, going from a 6th grade level to a 7th grade level in his listening ability. His vocabulary comprehension appears to be his weakest area. that is, selecting a word that does not belong with four other related words. When   started the year he was functioning with a 4th grade vocabulary comprehension level. When tested in March eh had progressed to a 6th grade level.

As in reading,   progress in Math has been significant as well. He started the year functioning on a 5th grade Math level and has progressed to a 6th grade level. His word problem reasoning skills appear to be on grade level. Completed the whole number piece of this Brigance assessment and he proved to be successful completing 75% of the problems without using a calculator. When given the opportunity to use his calculator, he was 100% successful. This assessment tested all four operations, up to an including 3 digits by 3 digits. In addition,   completed the decimal and the fraction component of the Brigance Test of Basic Skills. Again, he achieved 100% success with all four operations with decimals with a calculator and approximately 66% success with decimals without a calculator. As far as fractions is concerned, demonstrates ability to add, subtract and multiply like and unlike fractions.

In addition, to Reading and Math,   was tested in the area of English using the Brigance Test of Basic Skills. He progressed from a 5th grade level in spelling to as 6th grade level in spelling. He started the year functioning at a 5th grade level in sentence writing and ended the year on grade level in sentence writing as well.   has a basic understanding of what constitutes paragraph.

6

Hey, This Really Works!

State Test Results

All students in our state are required to take the Ohio Proficiency Test at various stages of their school career. Most states have their own version these days. Consequences are attached to specific pieces of this test along the way. For example, in fourth grade a student who doesn't pass the reading portion is expected to be retained for the year. This is known as the "Fourth Grade Guarantee." There are, of course, exceptions to this rule. All five parts of the Tenth Grade test must be passed in order for a student to receive a diploma. The student is invited to take the test more than once in an effort to pass, but if he doesn't ultimately pass he doesn't get a diploma. He will receive, instead, a certificate of attendance which states that he did, in fact, attend high school but didn't prove to be proficient in the curriculum. These are very high stakes. For a special education student struggling in the general curriculum, they are even higher.

Therefore, the state has allowed, in some circumstances, for these special education students to be exempt from the high stakes of these tests. That is, they could still receive a diploma even if they are not successful in passing the test. However, as you will see, special and regular education students who have participated in the inclusion unit have done very well on these tests. We have always had all the special education students who are participating in a coteaching model take the proficiency exam. This past year, 2003, marks the first time our state mandated that all students with special needs participate. The message is clear: "no child will be left behind."

With the new federal mandates in place, however, things have begun to change, including a bill that calls for "no child to be left behind." This includes our special education population. This makes a successful inclusion program even more inviting. Beginning in the year 2003 the state of Ohio mandated that no student would be exempt from the test. If students take it, their scores will be aggregated into the total and no exceptions will be made.

Throughout the state and the country, these proficiency tests have become a measuring stick to determine student progress and to gauge the success and quality of a particular school district. These scores are public information and are reported in the newspaper. Having said that, imagine the importance placed on these results and the pressure attached to these tests for students and teachers.

Having clarified this, it is with pride that I report the results of our students in the coteaching classroom. I have charted these results out in several ways so you can see them from different perspectives.

We have compiled results from the past three years, 2003, 2002 and 2001, which clearly chart the success of our program. The following pages contain these results.

The most exciting thing about these proficiency scores is that they get better each year. The 2003 tests are the best yet. Not only were our percentage passage rates considerably higher than the state standards, we had several special education students receive scores in the advanced proficient range. The following breaks down scores over five subject areas with the results for both populations.

In Writing class we had a total of 25 students this year. Seven were students with special needs and 18 were regular education. Every one of them passed our state proficiency test. In addition, two received scores in the advanced proficiency range as did eight typical students. Of the 28 students in Math this year, 25 passed the proficiency test, an 89% rate. Eight of 10 students with special needs passed as did 17 of 18 of the regular education students.

Of the 24 Science students, six had special needs. Five of six passed as did 16 of the 18 regular education students. One student with special needs received an advanced proficiency score and three others did as well. Although Reading has been our weakest area in the past, of 26 total students this year 25 passed, three students with special needs received an advanced proficient score as did 11 regular education students. Twenty-four students in our Social Studies inclusion class took the citizenship test, and 23 passed. One special education student received an advanced proficiency score as did six other students.

It's worth pointing out that in the Writing, Reading and Citizenship tests 100% of the regular education students passed.

Clearly sharing their learning experience with identified students hasn't slowed them down in any way.

Regular Education Students 2003				
Subject	Total Students	Number Passed	Number Failed	Percentage Passed
Writing	18	18	0	100%
Mathematics	18	17	1	94%
Science	18	16	2	89%
Reading	18	18	0	100%
Citizenship	18	18	0	100%

Special Education Students 2003				
Subject	Total Students	Number Passed	Number Failed	Percentage Passed
Writing	7	7	0	100%
Mathematics	10	8	2	80%
Science	6	5	1	83%
Reading	8	7	1	88%
Citizenship	6	5	1	83%

Next, we'll look at the inclusion class as a whole, combining all special education with regular education students and look at the scores as an entire class. Additionally, I am going to show you how the inclusion class compares to the other class that Kim and Karen teach alone, one with no identified children in attendance.

Entire Coteach Class Compared to Another Class 2003		
	Inclusion Class Success Rate	Other Class Success Rate
Writing	100%	86%
Mathematics	89%	86%
Science	88%	82%
Reading	96%	86%
Citizenship	96%	79%

In 2002, **every special education child passed at least three parts of the five part test**. There were a total of nine special education students in the inclusion program. Of those, five passed three parts, two passed four parts and two passed all five. In addition, one of the special education students who passed all five, also passed two of them with advanced proficient scores.

In writing, eight of nine special education students passed, while fifteen of the sixteen regular education students passed as well.

In citizenship, seven of nine special education students passed. The two who didn't had a raw score of 196 out of a needed 200. In citizenship, all sixteen regular education students passed – 100%.

In reading, two of nine special education students passed. Six of the seven who didn't were within 20 points of a passing score. This is significant because these special education students struggled in reading and in attending to task and these tests takes two and one half hours of sustained attention. These students put forth an enormous amount of effort. In reading, twelve of sixteen regular education students passed and four who didn't pass were within five points of a passing score. As you can see, reading presents the greatest struggle.

In math, all nine special education students passed, as did all sixteen regular education students passed. Our inclusion Math class achieved 100% passage. This has rarely been seen with a regular education class and never in an inclusion class.

In science, six of eight special education students passed and fourteen of sixteen regular education students. One of our special education students who passed this test got the highest science score in the school!

In the 2001 coteaching classroom, there was a total of 24 students, 14 were regular and 10 were identified students. Some of the students were learning or developmentally disabled and others emotionally disabled. First, the results of the 14 regular students, who have been learning and growing alongside students with special need on a daily basis.

Next, I will combine these groups and put results together into a class set. My 10 students add to the fourteen regular education students to make a class of twenty-four. I will then compare class scores of the coteaching model to those of

Regular Education Students 2002				
Subject	Total Students	Number Passed	Number Failed	Percentage Passed
Writing	16	15	1	94%
Mathematics	16	16	0	100%
Science	16	14	2	88%
Reading	16	12	4	75%
Citizenship	16	16	0	100%

Special Education Students 2002				
Subject	Total Students	Number Passed	Number Failed	Percentage Passed
Writing	9	8	1	89%
Mathematics	9	8	0	100%
Science	9	7	2	78%
Reading	9	2	7	22%
Citizenship	9	7	0	78%

Regular Education Students 2001				
Subject	Total Students	Number Passed	Number Failed	Percentage Passed
Writing	14	12	2	86%
Mathematics	14	13	1	93%
Science	14	11	3	79%
Reading	14	13	1	93%
Citizenship	14	13	1	93%

Special Education Students 2001				
Subject	Total Students	Number Passed	Number Failed	Percentage Passed
Writing	10	9	1	90%
Mathematics	10	7	3	70%
Science	10	6	4	60%
Reading	10	4	6	40%
Citizenship	10	8	2	80%

another set of children, all of whom are regular education students taught by the same two teachers.

Next, I would like to view these scores from an individual student basis. These results apply to special education students.

- 3 of the 10 special education students passed all five parts.

- 3 of 10 passed 4 of the 5 parts.

- 1 of 10 passed 3 of the 5 parts.

- 1 of 10 passed 2 of the 5 parts.
- 2 of 10 passed 1 of the 5 parts.

It is significant to point out that **all special education students passed at least one part of the test in the year 2001**. Also, two of these students passed one part of the test with an advanced proficient score. Of the fourteen regular education students, eleven passed all five parts. That is, 79%, experienced 100% success. Two of the remaining three students passed three of five parts and the final student passed one. These results make a substantial inference. The biggest complaint voiced about coteaching is that it's not fair to the regular education students. Some complain that with special education students in the classroom, the level of expectation and the degree of learning decreases. One can see from these results that's not the case. When this program is worked properly, it works for everyone.

In addition, if these special education students were still being educated apart from general education, they wouldn't have had the opportunity to take these tests. This echoes the sentiments of all conscientious educators, "set high standards for all students and help them achieve them. They will rise to the occasion."

These numbers speak for themselves. As you can see, when teachers and administrators understand the philosophy behind inclusion, believe in the success of all students, and can successfully implement it, everyone comes out a winner! No child should be left behind.

7

The Human Side of Inclusion

Anecdotal Information

When I was reviewing the statistics presented in Chapter Six with my administrator he asked me what I thought accounted for these success stories: The lift in self esteem for students with special needs, and the willingness of teachers to work together as a team, and treating all students fairly, if not all the same. I saw a sign once that said, "the most unfair thing to do to people is to treat them all the same."

When I reflect on the self esteem of our students with special needs, a few stories come to mind. The most recent one occurred within the last month.

TreShawn

Treshawn is a student with developmental disabilities who is a hard worker. He has given every ounce of effort any person could be expected to give. Being developmentally disabled, his IQ is somewhere below 80 and with 100 being the norm, he is trying to hold his own among students who are considerably more advanced than he. This student, however, was diligent about his work, and was willing to repeatedly redo his assignments until he improved his quality of work. As the end of the year drew near, I noticed that he began turning in work that was below what he had been doing. At first I didn't say anything because I thought he was exhausted, and understandably so. I didn't have the heart to say anything. I had already completed a pre-and post-test measuring his progress for the year and he had grown in all areas. So I sat back and let him coast for a while, until I noticed he had stopped working all together. I talked to him on repeated occasions, but to no avail. I also noticed that he began to get quiet, both in class and around his new friends. It seemed to me that overall he was not as happy nor as successful.

I had the IEP meeting scheduled with his mother, so I decided to wait and discuss my concerns with her. I told her how much I admired his outstanding work ethic and that they should be proud of the progress he had made. She had tears in her eyes as she said, "there's just one thing that my son wants me to ask. He doesn't want to go into that dark hallway next year. He is afraid of that place." We have a wing in our school where the lights seem to burn out quicker than in the rest of the building. There must be something wrong with the wiring in that part of the building, but for whatever reason, the bulbs need to be changed often in that wing. As diligent as our janitor is, the hallway does tend to be a little dark. Coincidently, two of our three special education classes are housed there. This boy had been in class with many of these students prior to inclusion and he feared he was going to be put back in the self-contained room at "the end of the dark hall." I emphasized to her that he had worked hard and had grown and was going to remain in the general curriculum. He was not up to grade level, and may never be, but his rate of growth was phenomenal. I ended the meeting, assuming that she would reassure her son.

But, his behavior didn't change. After a few days, I asked him if his mom had spoken to him after our meeting. He said she had but he wasn't sure what she had meant. I said, "Honey, you are not going to go into that dark hall." With that, his face lit up. The next day, he came back to school with his homework done and he had clearly spent hours on computer back-work I had given up on. The next day he handed it all in and asked if he could come up and work with me during his study hall because there were a few things he needed help on.

There is another related story I want to share with you.

Last year our janitor installed name plates above all the classrooms in the school. Below mine it said "Special Needs Teacher." I was so busy going about my daily routines, I didn't notice it until a student pointed it out to me. It had upset him terribly.

I was walking back from lunch a few days later, when the nurse called me into her office. This student had gone to the nurse's office daily for medication and she noticed a change in his usual friendly personality. Through a conversation with him she discovered that since he knew what "Special Needs Teacher" meant, he assumed I must be his teacher. If I was his teacher, then this meant that he was a student with special needs. A friend told him that meant retarded. He was devastated and so was I. A simple oversight caused this child's world to be rocked. Through repeated dialogue with him, my partner teachers and myself were able to get him back on his feet again. Naturally, the name plates were changed immediately.

Jimmy

Jimmy was a student of mine when I taught in a self-contained unit before the days of inclusion. Jimmy was socially competent and aware of being in a special class. His friends were regular education students. He was athletic and a member of the football team. He was embarrassed by being in a special class and tried hard to hide it from his friends. Every day he walked up and down the hall outside my room waiting for it to clear. When no one remained in the hall, he entered class. This made him late for every class. I knew what he was doing and said nothing of his being late. I also noticed he was doing the same thing at the bus stop. He rode a "special bus" because he was a special education student and didn't want his friends to know. This poor child spent a large part of his day focusing on how to hide his disabilities. We, as school personnel, only highlighted his disabilities to the rest of his peers. Needless to say, he was not successful. If he wasn't hiding his disability, he was asking me how he could get out of this class. He would have been a perfect candidate for inclusion had this program been around when he was at our school.

Juanita

All teachers have students who touch their hearts and remain with them for a lifetime, validating why they went into teaching. For me, it was Juanita. She was diagnosed special education at an early age and was serviced primarily in self-contained classrooms until she came to me in sixth grade.

Juanita joined our sixth grade inclusion class a few weeks into the school year. Her family had moved into our district and didn't begin school until the middle of September. Juanita was a lonely, anxious little girl who had changed schools often. She had serious issues surrounding self-esteem and confidence. Her feeling of insecurity and often manifested as anger. Consequently, she had frequent outbursts in the classroom which frustrated teachers and alienated classmates. The prospect of her being "included" seemed minimal.

If we were going to help Juanita, we had to establish a trusting relationship. The first order of business was to study her behavior and find out what her triggers were; when was she losing control. We spent the first weeks observing and charting behaviors. This gave us a baseline to begin discussion with Juanita.

We noticed that when she had a bad day it started in homeroom and got worse as the day went on. Initially, when Juanita had an outburst of anger she ran out of the room and through the school building until she found a place to hide. She would stay there until we found her. We also noticed that these "escapes" always followed an incident in which Juanita received detention or late assignment notices that needed to be signed by her parents. One day I sat with her in a far corner of an empty classroom as she cried harder than I thought was possible. She told us the severe punishments she received when her parents received notices of incomplete work or inappropriate behavior. If she asked her parents for help with her homework, they punished her for that too.

While this information is confidential, readers should know that we involved Health and Human Services, who took appropriate measures, including insuring that she stay at our school for the remainder of the year. Also, the last we'd heard, the family was still engaged in counseling on their recommendation.

After reporting this to the proper authorities, the first thing we had to do was prevent her from running through the school and hiding in various places. This behavior was dangerous and I had to come up with a reasonable compromise with Juanita. When she got scared her urge to run was too strong to expect it to extinguish completely so we had to come up with workable modifications. I explained to Juanita why she couldn't run and hide. While she was diagnosed as an student with emotionally disabilities she had a normal intelligence level. Her emotions often interfered with her learning but she understood basic logic. Together we worked out the following plan.

When Juanita got upset, her fuse was short but she had some foreknowledge. So, we set up a table and chair outside the classroom. We designated it as home base. When Juanita felt the urge to run, she could run to the table, but no further. When her anxiety level was accelerated, Juanita could not express herself. She had to remove herself and have time to cool down. These "time outs" were necessary when she was working in a small group in class and things weren't going her way, or when she was overwhelmed by something or if she had had a bad morning before school. Whatever was making her upset, this was a quick fix to circumvent her panicked outbursts. But, this was just a short term solution. We needed to establish a social skills program to help her deal with her negative emotions in a healthy way. As a team, counselors, administrators, and teachers we found time in her schedule to fit this program in. Additionally, we found other students who benefited from a course like this.

During this class Juanita kept a journal she often shared with me. Students could choose to keep the journal at school or carry it back and forth from school to home. Juanita chose to keep it at school.

This created a safe pathway for her to express her feelings and know there was no threat attached to her communication. In addition, the journal served as a great teaching tool for me and my fellow teachers. Often we were able to see through her journal writings ways she could make things better for herself. So it served a dual purpose. In addition, through this social skills class, Juanita learned tools she could implement at home to help de-escalate emotions.

Once we got these immediate emotional needs met, we turned our attention to helping Juanita become successful academically. As with most special education students, her behavior had seriously impacted her academic progress. Consequently, there were many gaps in her learning that needed to be addressed. Anxiety was at the forefront of these problems.

In English, essay writing was an activity she found overwhelming. She needed more structure than she could get from a blank piece of paper. It was mandatory that when writing was addressed with the class that either myself or my partner work with Juanita until her pre-write activity was completed. Sometimes we worked on an outline and other times we created a web. Once this was finished, she was able to begin on her rough draft by herself. She had to know, however, that if she got stuck or confused that one of us would come to her desk as quickly as possible to further assist her. Once she completed her rough draft, we edited it with her to help model proofreading and editing skills. When there was a breakdown in this process, things would get tense. But as time went on and Juanita knew she could trust us to be there for her, her anxiety level slowly began to decrease.

But, anxiety remained a real issue for Juanita. Dictated spelling tests that were built around a time frame were not helpful in assessing her. Therefore, we gave her multiple choice spelling tests with an unlimited time frame.

Like English, Math class posed a problem. She had difficulty transferring word problems into math calculation problems. We made modification math sheets available to her and she was able to participate successfully. She was instructed to go home and complete as much math independently as possible. Any problems she struggled with, she was to circle and see us in the morning. When she came to us that next day, we found time to help her with those problems before math class. That way she felt comfortable walking into math class prepared.

Juanita was probably my most challenging student. Maybe that is why she holds such a soft spot in my heart. I can't explain how rewarding it was to watch her settle down over the course of the year and begin to blend in. Watching her build friendships with other regular education students reaffirmed for me the value of inclusion. Everyone wants to belong, and everyone wants to be accepted for who they are.

Juanita left our school after that year. Her family moved again. She called me from her new school during teacher appreciation week to thank me. She said, "I have never had anyone like me as much as you did." She said things were getting better at home because she was learning how to deal with her situation better. I cried after that call.

Tommy

Tommy was a student with developmental disabilities who had spent most of his school career in a self-contained intervention class. He was socially aware and like Jimmy, didn't want anyone to know he was being taught in special education classes. He was on the football team and most of his friends were in regular education. When he first arrived at our school as a sixth grader, his IEP team determined that his placement be in a self-contained class. I was his teacher.

As a result, he became apathetic. Behavior issues began to arise. Finally, we called a conference with his parents to see if we could get to the bottom of the problem. During the conference his parents told us his feelings about being isolated from the rest of the student body and asked if it was possible to change his IEP and try him in an inclusion class. We agreed putting him in even one class he could be successful in would raise his self-esteem and eliminate many of the problems he was experiencing. Math was his strongest subject, so we put him in an inclusion math class. He worked very hard in there. He was even willing to come to school early to receive tutoring when things got tough. In the inclusion class, he met a girl who started to write him notes. This was awkward for Tommy because writing was difficult for him. He was aware of his disability and feared that if he wrote back she might make fun of him. On the other hand, if he didn't write back, she might not like him. Since we had built his trust and he believed we wanted to help him be successful, he brought the notes to us and asked us to help. We did and from then on he was accepted as one of the gang. The following year he was placed in a full inclusion unit and remained successful. He came back to visit me a short time ago, and has started his own lawn care company and is successful. He said he will never forget how we "helped him make friends." He believes that once he began to feel a part of the school, he was willing to work and therefore become successful.

Cheryl

Cheryl was a sweet, conscientious student who wanted very much to be successful in her school work. She was the opposite of Tommy and Jimmy and very much feared inclusion classes. She was afraid they would be too hard and she would fail. She had been in regular education classes up to third grade, when tests found her to be a student with learning disabilities. She was placed in an intervention unit for fourth and fifth grade. In these classes she was very successful. She came to me in sixth grade, and was placed in my self-contained unit. There she worked very hard and was successful. Our school had just begun to implement inclusion and I knew she would succeed in this setting. So, for her seventh grade placement the IEP team placed her in the inclusion unit. She and her mother were fearful due to past struggles they had experienced. As her teacher, however, I had witnessed her strong work ethic and believed that given the chance and support in the general curriculum, she had the potential to be successful. After much discussion we placed Cheryl in the unit. We assured her that all the teachers would be in constant communication about her success and if she felt intimidated at all, to talk honestly to us. With this safety net in place, she seemed to feel comfortable enough to give it a try.

As expected, she was successful academically and socially. By the end of the first quarter, she was gaining confidence and was happy as a result. Her seventh- and eight-grade experiences were positive. She moved on to high school in our district and experienced the same success there as well.

After a year or two of high school, I received the letter above from her.

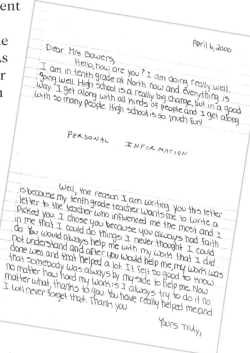

April 6, 2000

Dear Mrs Bowers,
   Hello, how are you? I am doing really well. I am in tenth grade at North now and everything is going well. High school is a really big change, but in a good way. I get along with all kinds of people and I get along with so many people. High school is so much fun!

PERSONAL   INFORMATION

   Well, the reason I am writing you this letter is because my tenth grade teacher wants me to write a letter to the teacher who influenced me the most and I picked you. I chose you because you always had faith in me that I could do things I never thought I could do. You would always help me with my work that I did not understand and after you would help me, my work was done well and that helped a lot. It felt so good to know that somebody was always by my side to help me. Now no matter how hard my work is I always try to do it no matter what, thanks to you. You have really helped me and I will never forget that. Thank you.

                    Yours Truly,

Cheryl's letter

Summary

When we look back to our own school days we don't recall specific lessons, science experiments or participating in projects. We do, however, recall how we felt when we were in school, how we were treated by peers and teachers. These feelings, in part, led us to become the person we are today. Our feelings about those times drive our actions and beliefs about ourselves. Sometimes as professionals we get so caught up in 'what' we are teaching that we forget 'who' we are teaching. The 'who' part is more powerful and impacting on our students lives. For children in middle school, being a part of the group, accepted by your peers is extremely important. They don't want to feel different or "special" in any way. They want to be like everybody else in as many ways as possible. I went to a high school reunion a few years ago. When we got there, they gave us a copy of the graduation picture that appeared in our yearbook. They made it into a pin, which we wore beside our name tag. As I moved through the evening, visiting with various classmates, I noticed how much all the girl's pictures looked alike. We all tried so hard to look like everyone else. We wanted to fit in and none of us wanted to stand out. As adolescents the need to belong is strong and we need to acknowledge it as we help them reach toward adulthood. We can teach all students and help in their overall development if we take a careful, sensitive approach to inclusion. Since the inception of inclusion, year after year we have students saying things like, "I need a little extra help with this work because I used to be L.D."

Sometimes as professionals we get so caught up in 'what' we are teaching that we forget 'who' we are teaching.

This statement proves to us that in their thinking, their label was gone. They were finally just like everyone else. To us, this means success.

Watching them become an accepted part of their peer group is a huge piece of the Inclusion Program. It brings about successful social growth, which is a huge piece of healthy development. After spending a year together in a coteach classroom, we see special education students become best friends with students who are members of the national junior honors society. They have not been told, nor do they care,

about academic differences. They are middle school students going through life together.

Karen Finnegan, a regular education teacher, when asked to share her feelings about the Inclusion Program, notes:

"In years past, students were made to feel 'dumb' or 'stupid' or inferior to their classmates because they were pulled out to get tutoring or sent to a special class. The beauty of inclusion is that needs of individuals can be met in the classroom. The stigma of being different is eliminated. An effective inclusion classroom allows for the individual needs of students to be met in such a way that others are unaware of modifications or adaptations.

"Learning modalities need to be considered when planning any lesson. When planning for an inclusion classroom, educators need to be focused on teaching so students can use various learning modalities. Often a single lesson will include a combination of learning modalities. An effective teacher in an inclusion classroom knows the strong modalities or learning style of her students and is able to adjust a lesson so kids are learning, using their strengths while developing strength in the other modalities."

Parents, too, want their child to be happy and successful. They want their children to grow up with good self-esteem and be accepted by others. They want their needs to be met, but not at the expense of their self-esteem. When we work together as a team with the child at the forefront, it's a win-win for everyone involved.

During open house we explain to parents our class structure and how we run our inclusion class. We outline for them the individual differences and how we deal with them. We are careful, however, to make certain no students are present in the classroom when we address these issues. If students come with their parents, we send them on an errand at that point. We explain to parents that every child will not be treated the same, but they will be treated fairly. We encourage parents to call us if their children come home complaining that one student got something they didn't. Over the years we have found that the majority of parents like their children being involved in an inclusion class.

When we address students in the beginning of the year, explaining classroom rules and expectations, we also address differences they will find in our classroom. We are open about the fact that people learn differently and that since they are lucky enough to have two teachers, they can receive twice as much help. We talk about how students "learn through their ears" and how others "learn through their eyes." Therefore, some students prefer to take a test having someone read it to them, whereas others would rather be left alone in a quiet room to read the test to themselves. We tell the class we are lucky because we (my partner and I) are good friends and since we ran out of classrooms, our principal let us work together in the same room. We try to create a "different strokes for different folks" atmosphere in our classroom, an atmosphere that leads to the success of all students.

8

And For You Administrators . . .

Suggested Method for Leading
Special Education Teachers
in the Coteaching Model

This concept of inclusion is still pretty new and its
interpretations are many. As an administrator, you may have
to assist teachers in coming to some kind of schoolwide
consensus on what inclusion should look like and how best to
organize its implementation.

Step #1:

What does inclusion look like

Hold a staff meeting and explain the philosophy of a coteaching classroom. Ask teachers to share ideas and come to some type of consensus on how the entire staff can best serve students in an inclusive setting. Discuss how to "team teach" and to determine who is responsible for what.

Step #2:

A profile of a successful inclusion student

Explain that inclusion is just one more placement on the continuum of services within special education. Inclusion is not the appropriate placement for every special education student. Give the staff criteria I have used in the past to determine who would be successful in this type of setting: As a school, work toward educating all special education students in the least restrictive environment that is the most appropriate in advancing the personal development of each. Always remember, too, to look at what is best for that particular student, not necessarily what the teacher would prefer.

Step #3:

Define Accommodations and Modifications

Explain the difference between the terms. An accommodation is when you "adjust" or "supplement" the curriculum to meet a child's needs. A modification is when you "change" or "alter" the curriculum to meet the child's needs. An example of an accommodation would be allowing a student to use a skeletal set of notes, orally reading to him or putting words or a book on tape to accommodate an auditory learning modality. For modification, however, you would eliminate higher level questions from the curriculum, or institute a grade curving plan to allow him to compete in the general education class. In essence, you don't hold the child responsible for all learner outcomes. It needs to be pointed out here that substantial modifications to the curriculum may allow for students to be exempt from statewide high stakes proficiency tests (as it is with the Ohio Proficiency Test), accommodations DO NOT!

Step #4:

Strategies for the coteaching model

Make available for the staff, either individually or as a group, specific possible strategies that could be used with individual students with special needs in the inclusive classroom. I sat with my special needs teachers to review student IEPs and from there adopted accommodations and modifications that made those children successful. Hopefully, this would be an ongoing review, as you and the teacher touch base throughout the year checking on the progress of your students.

Step #5:

Forms for documentation

Share with the staff two forms designed to assist in documentation and placement of special needs students: Academic Snapshot (Chapter Five, pg. 83) and Educational Prescription (Chapter Five, pg.86). Using the Brigance Diagnostic Test of Basic Skills, demonstrate how to use the Snapshot. Once this is completed, demonstrate how to use the Prescription. These forms would remain in the student's file for the remainder of the year as working documents. Throughout the year, jot down the status of a particular accommodation/modification — that is, whether it's successful for the student or not. At the conclusion of the year, re-test the student with the same assessment tool and compare results from the beginning to the end of the year. Each teacher should individualize these forms to best meet students needs. The forms here are primarily for middle and high school students.

Step #6:

Create a file for every special education student

Advise the special education teachers to set up individual files for each student. Begin the year with their IEPs, an Academic Snapshot filled out with current year opening information and a completed Educational Prescription. With this plan in action, encourage the teacher to begin compiling work to establish some type of portfolio for the student to be used as an assessment at the year's end. Any correspondence with parents or other institutions can be held in these files. Upon the completion of the year, conduct a second Academic Snapshot to compare progress from beginning to end of year.

Step #7:

Regular special education teacher responsibilities

In meeting with the teacher team, inform and discuss who is responsible for what. This is a springboard to get the discussion started. Have all teachers draw up their responsibilities and expectations so they may own them and carry them out. Follow-up meetings may be needed to bring closure to some type of overall understanding of the direction the team is heading.

Meet with them on a regular basis, possibly quarterly. At that time, discuss:

- Comfort level of teachers in this setting and brainstorm ways to improve this.

- Progress of students by examining initial Snapshots and following through to the modifications and accommodations listed on the Prescriptions.

- Examination of student portfolios to see concrete evidence of accommodations and modifications and see if any necessary adjustments need to be made.

The goal of the coteaching inclusive classrooms is to make every child feel as though they belong. Distinctions should not be made publicly between special needs and regular education students. Therefore, many of these modifications and accommodations need to be delivered with discretion. Sensitively make these students aware of their disabilities and teach them how to live with and work around them. We must be careful not to enable or make excuses for them.

Self-esteem is a huge piece of the success level of any student in the classroom. When implementing accommodations and modifications, never forget you're handling a child who wants to be like everyone else and accepted as 'one of the group.' Walk gently and guard your task carefully.

During the process of completing this work, I interviewed special and regular education teachers working in a coteach situation. I asked them what they expected from their partner teachers. Attached are the results of the surveys.

Summary Results for Regular Education

The following is what the regular education teachers expect of the special education teachers they work with.

- They will equally share planning and teaching responsibilities.

- They equally share all responsibilities of the classroom.

- They will teach lessons together.

- They should coteach on a daily basis.

- There should not be a visible difference to students between the regular and the special education teachers.

- The special educator assists in lesson planning.

- They work together 100% of the time on every lesson.

Summary Results for Special Education

The following is what special education teachers expect of the regular education teachers they work with.

- They provide a copy of the test at least two days in advance so the special education teacher can make modifications.

- They provide a copy of worksheets at least two days in advance so that the special education teacher can make modifications.

- Provide a copy of overhead notes at least two days in advance so that the special education teacher can make a skeletal set of notes for some students.

- They provide open and ongoing communication with the special education teacher about problems and concerns with any student in the class to make for a "team" approach in teaching and classroom management.

- They share cooperative planning time to develop lessons which are inclusive of all students. This ensures a positive environment for the entire class. On occasion, when cooperative planning doesn't occur, lessons should be shared by Friday of the week prior to instruction.

- They offer an agreed-upon location for the storage of materials and lessons so that either teacher can fill in for one another at any given time.

- That a mutual respect be shown by both teachers to each other for their individual area of expertise.

9

Relationship Dynamics

Building Working Relationships Between Coteachers

Middle school is a tough time for kids and they often make sure their teachers share their struggles with them. It can be an even worse experience when the child is a special education student who is segregated from his peers in a self-contained classroom.

In the time I have been involved in building our inclusion program over the past half decade, I have seen my fair share of disagreements, including conflicting teaching styles. Sometimes, it's necessary to halt the process and sit down and iron out these problems. This chapter puts forth a conflict resolution approach that may help you deal with these frictions and go on to start an inclusionary program that works for everyone involved, from the administration to instructional staff to the students. The effectiveness of any model work plan depends on the people who carry it out. At Eastlake Middle School in Eastlake, Ohio and at Bessie Weller Elementary School in Staunton, Virginia, the inclusion model works because teachers understand and are committed to the value of inclusion and the benefits of a collaborative two-teacher method. The administrative team supports the program, communicates this to staff, and works continually to assist them in any way that is needed.

The inclusion program requires a clear statement of purpose and clear working guidelines, as found in this book. It needs administrative and staff support, and a good working relationship between the classroom and special education teachers. The working relationship is key. We can have excellent procedures and external support, but if there is not good teamwork between the two teachers who work with the students day in and day out, the program will struggle and all of the students under the care of the two teachers will not be served.

Collaboration can be smooth and effective or it can be difficult and ineffective. In this chapter we will look at some of the difficulties and successes that people experience when working together and explore different ways to build a good working relationship primarily between regular and special educators, as well as the principal and other involved staff.

Working Relationships

The Life of the Organization/School

The workplace is a collection of working relationships. Schools, corporations, government agencies can all show an organizational chart which describes the power, authority, reporting and responsibility structures of the organization. It can be a splendid, artistic, graphic creation designed to show the connections of departments and functions. But what is not shown on the chart is the human dynamic of working relationships. An excellent structure rests in the hands of the people who implement it. The productivity of the school or company, is, in the end, a product of the people and how they work together.

Often Overlooked

In our schools, working relationships are simply expected to work. Teachers are professionals. That means accepting the direction of supervisors and carrying out those duties in an effective, efficient manner. The completion of the task is the goal. It may require working with others to accomplish the task, and it's expected that any working relationship will work. If it doesn't, it's the fault of the teachers.

Not much attention is given to the working relationship in schools. The hiring and orientation process for new employees is focused more on talent, knowledge, expertise, schedules and organizational charts than on the interaction of the players on the team. In schools not much time is given to orienting new staff, novice or veteran. They receive little direction and must ask their own questions to gain helpful knowledge that could be answered in a simple, insightful orientation program. A lot is given over to chance this way. Much time is lost. Unnecessary tensions and conflicts arise from assumptions, misunderstanding, lack of knowledge and confusion. Conflicts which could have been prevented arise unnecessarily.

Forming – Storming – Norming – Performing

A common experience in working groups at schools and in other workplaces is a process of forming, storming, norming and performing.

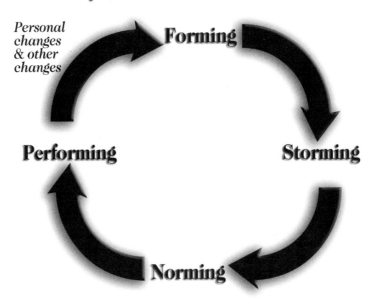

A Dynamic of Teamwork

Personal changes & other changes

Forming

Storming

Norming

Performing

Forming

In the forming phase, a new working group starts up. It may be an orchestra, a basketball team, a marketing department for a company or a regular and a special education inclusion team. Everything is new. The entire team may consist of people who have not met or worked together before. It may be a mix of continuing staff and newcomers. Some will be older, some younger. The make-up of the group is a collection of known and unknown experiences, knowledge, preferences, expertise and styles.

Storming

In the storming phase, the personalities and styles of the group go through an initial upheaval process. People begin to work together on projects. They agree and disagree. There is smooth sailing, there is conflict. Some are shy observers at first, while others are outspoken from the start. Some assert their ideas, knowledge, opinions, methods and patterns attempting to have others follow their lead. In this phase people find where things fit and what works. They discover what causes friction, what creates obstacles to the group's work, what is incompatible; what causes conflicts, and how they can be resolved.

Norming

After a while, patterns develop. Everyone begins to see how they fit in and how they can contribute, how they can work together and how things operate. They settle into a normalcy, honing effective teamwork and reducing ineffective patterns. Eventually the members of the group and the work process itself begins to flow. Performance and productivity increase as norms are understood and followed. The team becomes efficient, effective and productive.

Performing

In the performance phase, the team has gotten it right. They have learned to move with each other's thoughts and patterns. The group accomplishes tasks and completes projects as a matter of course, without the confusion and extra effort of the storming phase. Performance becomes simple and yields results.

Changes and Recycling

The performance phase continues until an unexpected change occurs. A team member may leave, or a new player may be hired or transferred in. The group must reform, storm and norm again. This may be effortless or it may be traumatic. Each year, for example, a basketball team has different personnel, which means new levels of known and unknown experiences, knowledge, preferences, expertise and styles.

An Example of F-S-N-P

Each year a basketball team must come together anew to form, storm, norm and perform. Success happens at different times for different teams. One team may be smooth early in the season, able to defeat many opponents in the opening weeks. Another team may struggle for half the season, but in the final weeks they begin to perform. Their season record is only average and they receive a low placement in end-of-season tournaments. The press predicts they will not reach the second round. But they are reaching their performance phase and make it all the way to the finals. They are called the surprise team, the Cinderellas, because they seem to have had a sudden transformation. In reality, it was a normal process which took the whole season.

The School Inclusion Team

The regular and special education teachers come together as an inclusion team. They will likely go through a storming phase, getting to know each other. Eventually they will settle into a norming phase where things are more predictable. Eventually they will evolve into the performing stage where efforts and thoughts are complementary.

If the team can come together in a facilitated or planned partnering process, they can speed up the getting acquainted time and overcome many of these hurdles through communication and problem-solving up front. The process of partnering will be discussed later in this chapter.

Difficulties of Working Together in the Inclusion Model

Sometimes collaboration is difficult for teachers who are working together in the inclusion model. In this chapter we will look at some of the difficulties that teachers experience working together and explore different ways to build a good working relationship. When working together each teacher may need to make some adjustments including:

1. More planning time to coordinate for two.

2. Having to live and work with another person closely.

3. Not always being able to chose the other teacher.

4. Communicating regularly with a partner.

5. Developing and maintaining good working relationships.

When people feel heard in a decision-making process or discussion, they are more accepting of the outcome. When people have expertise or a stake in the outcome, they often feel resentful and resistant when told what to do without being asked or consulted. For example, state highway departments have long been criticized for telling communities where and how they planned to build a road. Without including the community in the conversation and the planning, they are met by a great deal of public resistance and resentment for long periods of time. They gained less than desirable reputations.

Today, highway departments spend many months and even years informing a community of their interest in building a road and explaining why. Then they hold forums to hear from community citizens and business people to learn their thoughts and concerns. From these information sessions and discussions, the department will modify the original road plan to meet the wishes of the community. Together local citizens and department officials design it. As a result of this collaborative process, highway departments have reduced the amount of public resentment and resistance to their road projects.

These same issues crop up among school staff. When teachers receive a directive from the principal ordering them to carry out a new program or policy when they haven't participated in the planning, it is often met with resentment and resistance. The implementation is carried out by disgruntled staff members who will dutifully comply but may not put much enthusiasm and creativity into the process. When the implementers involved in the planning, they are usually more enthusiastic, committed, creative and effective in carrying it out.

Collaborative planning is necessary for the inclusion team to succeed in teaching all students. A respectful working relationship in which the teachers invite each other to contribute their knowledge, opinions and ideas will serve the team well in at least two ways:

1. They express helpful information and insightful analysis which will form a strong basis for plans and decisions.

2. They have both participated in planning, problem-solving and decision making which will make them more able and willing to implement their plans.

Control

Some people have difficulty delegating tasks or working with others because:

1. It's a new process and requirement.

2. They feel they no longer control the process and the outcome.

We Are Often Not Prepared for Conflict

For many people conflict is uncomfortable. Administrators and team leaders often don't talk openly about it. They avoid this sensitive topic because they don't know how to handle it. They don't want to hurt anyone's feelings, or they are afraid that once mentioned the conflict will be too difficult to handle and may get out of control. They hope it will solve itself or go away. They don't have a plan nor do they have the training or experience to work through sensitive issues, manage conflict and effectively move to conflict resolution.

The result is that conflict occurs without a method or system for dealing with it in a constructive, productive way. It festers. It's talked around but not about. The people who need to be talking to each other aren't. The conflict is real. If it's not managed well, it will impair working relationships because people begin to shut down communication on important work related topics. It can cause a rift in the staff when people side with one or the other and stress in staff members who are connected to the conflict. Staff performance and student achievement may be compromised.

Makes people uncomfortable

Normal part of the human experience

Has a negative image

Conflict

Need to be comfortable & capable

An opportunity for:
learning
understanding
resolution
moving on
reducing stress
growth
justice

Normal part of the workplace

Conflict Presents Opportunities

Consider the following questions:

1. How many times have you had conflict with anyone?

2. Have you had conflict with the same person more than once?

3. Have you ever seen conflict in your workplace?

Ask these questions of yourself, your friends and colleagues. You will find that the answer to each question is yes. Conflict is a normal part of the human experience.

Whenever two or more people come together, there is the potential for different ideas, disagreement, argument and conflict. There is also the opportunity for new ideas, creativity, progress and success.

Conflict management is an important part of organizational life, but it is often overlooked in our colleges, management training courses and workplace orientation programs. Breathing is normal, so we learn about air quality and respiration to keep us healthy. Eating is normal, so we learn about nutrition and digestion to keep us healthy. Conflict is normal, but we often ignore it and get ourselves into unhealthy situations.

Perception

1. We act from what we know, think, think we know, or assume, from confusion or from fear.

2. We know what we have learned, from our perceptions.

3. Our perceptions are based on our experiences, our knowledge, our interests and our motivations.

4. Perception is reality.

Culture

5. Cultural differences of gender, race, age, ethnicity, religion, nationality, locality, etc. affect the way we see the world, our expectations, comforts, confidences and fears.

Fear

6. Conflict comes from confusion, misunderstanding and fear.

7. Conflict can go unresolved if one is comfortable and does not see or care about the concerns of the other.

Expectations

8. Conflict comes from expectations unmet.

9. Conflict comes from expectations unspoken.

10. Conflict comes from expectations that differ.

Resolution and Forgiveness

11. Resolution comes from understanding.

12. Resolution comes from realizing the benefit of resolution.

13. Forgiveness is not automatic.

14. Forgiveness can begin by first telling the truth.

Change

15. Change begets conflict.

16. Those who suggest or implement change are often comfortable with the change. They have taken time to think it through. They see the benefits or inevitability of the change. They do not understand and may become impatient with question and resistance.

17. Those who are having change put upon them by others without previous knowledge or participation, are often not comfortable with the change. They have not had, nor taken time, to think it through. They do not see the benefits or acceptability or inevitability of the change. They are likely to question and resist.

18. Dealing with change is a process similar to grieving: Denial – Anger-Exploration – Acceptance.

Normal — An Opportunity

Conflict is a normal part of human existence:	Conflict is often based on:
change	a threat to comfort
fear of the unknown	a threat to power
misunderstanding	a threat to position
lack of communication or poor communication	a threat to job status
expectations unmet	a threat to job security
expectations unspoken	
not being part of decision-making that affects our lives	
feelings of disrespect or exclusion	
reduced responsibility	
unclear job role	
unclear job expectations	

19. Conflict is a normal part of the human experience and certainly a part of the workplace experience.

20. We can make it an opportunity for something good.

These elements may be present in the teaming of two teachers for inclusion of special education students.

If the general educator was not part of the decision to team with a special educator, the conflict may rest with the lawmakers or policy makers who forced this upon them. This is simple change, and all of the feelings and adjustments that are required for that can be problematic.

Including the two teachers in the planning may make it easier for them to implement the team teaching approach. Introducing students with different learning styles and abilities and some adjustments for the classroom teacher. The teacher may feel she is going to have to handle these children alone. But remember the presence of the special education teacher; an active participant and skilled educator, a great resource.

Becoming Comfortable and Capable

Conflict is normal and is going to occur in our daily lives. It's going to happen with the inclusion team. Team members and their supervisors must become comfortable with conflict and capable at achieving resolution in order to productively deal with each other, with students and with parents in stressful situations.

Conflict is an opportunity for learning, understanding, positive change, trust building, resolution, restoration and many other helpful experiences.

For teachers and administrators to productively work with the interpersonal aspects of the inclusion team, they need knowledge, skills and methods:

- Knowledge of conflict and teamwork

- Skills in listening and problem-solving

- Methods to plan for and to manage conflict as it arises

The following pages provide some valuable knowledge, skills and methods to enhance the effectiveness of the inclusion team's planning, teamwork and performance for success.

Expectations, Assumptions and Roles

School expectations for the principal, the team and each of its member should be clearly stated and written down. This will serve to head off conflict, inform decision, guide actions, help each person understand the motivation and reaction of each other.

Expectations unmet are a common cause of misunderstanding and conflict. Expectations unspoken compound the problem and are another common source of problems. For example, consider a mother whose daughters came to visit. They commented that she wasn't wearing her diamond ring. She said the diamond had been lost and she couldn't find it. They suggested she replace it. she said "That's for your father to do." They asked if she had told him of her expectation. "No, " she replied, "he should know." This unspoken expectation became the source of tension and conflict for the entire family.

When people work together they act on what they know combined with what they assume. Sometimes assumptions are based on good information and acting on them can be helpful. Other times assumptions are based on hopes or myths and, when acted upon, cause problems.

An open discussion of expectations, assumptions and roles, early in the life of the team, make for a smooth and effective operation. An ongoing discussion of expectations, assumptions and roles every few weeks or months will keep everyone informed and create understanding between co-workers.

Change

Change is a common cause of conflict. Change affects people in different ways. Dealing with change is similar to the grieving process. People are initially in denial that a change has occurred. Then they experience strong emotion and anger about it. They learn and explore what the change means to them and what they must do next. Finally, they reach for acceptance of the change. It may be reluctantly, but they have come to grips with the new reality.

Let's compare these phases of denial, anger, exploration and acceptance for someone who has lost a loved one and for the classroom teacher who has been told she will participate in an inclusion program.

Change in the workplace is not an easy thing for people. The principal who announces the beginning of an inclusion plan has gone through the change process in his thinking by the time he brings it to the staff who will implement the program. So, he's surprised at their questions and resistance. After all, he has thought it through and even received direction from the superintendent. It makes sense to him.

When people are at different stages in the change process, it can cause confusion and conflict. Informing people early, and including the implementers in the program development process, is effective in having them buy into the program and to implement it well.

Misunderstandings: From Unclear Statements, Assumptions, Lack of Knowledge

Communication is a tricky process. Misunderstandings often come from unclear statements and different assumptions.

Television advertisers say that it takes eight "hits" of a commercial before the viewer even knows what the product is. They are in the business of communicating ideas: They know communication requires clarity and repetition. We must take responsibility that clear communication is taking place.

Styles of Communication and Conflict Resolution

People communicate and handle conflict in different ways at different times based on experience, age, gender, race, culture, height, nationality, locality, religion, socialization and other elements of our many different realities. Below are some descriptions of some of the ways people communicate and respond to conflict.

Debate VS. Dialogue. Competition VS. Collaboration.

We live and work in a very competitive society. Competition is the nature of our capitalistic economy. It is in our schools. We see it on the sports fields, in our classrooms, and on report cards. We talk about competitive admission to colleges and competitive classes of honors students.

Our entertainment is based on competitive games from football, to track and field, to Wheel of Fortune, to checkers. Our children compete to get to the water fountain first in elementary school. Customers race to get to the check-out counter ahead of the next person. We use words like "first, best, favorite, right, only and highest" to describe our goals in life, our grades on a test, our opinions and our shoes.

Our culture is one of constant comparisons. We are constantly asking or telling which is better; this car, this sandwich, this school, or this teacher.

Debate

We even compete when we simply talk to each other. We talk about a topic to win the conversation. We jockey for position in the group discussion by making some important statement about the subject at hand or by passing it off as unimportant. We start out with an opinion and spend the whole meeting trying to prove ourselves right and attempting to win others over to our side. We are fixed on debate and competitive conversation. But on the inclusion team, using the debating style to discuss tomorrow's lesson plans often creates and maintains a competitive, distrustful tension between teachers.

Debate Focuses On:

speaking	not listening
telling	not learning
winning	not understanding
impressing	not informing
win-lose	not win-win
me	not all of us
being right	not being informed
finding flaws in another's ideas	listening to another's point of view

Dialogue

Dialogue is a non-competitive method of communication that is based on learning all points of view in order to make a good, informed decision. It is respectful of those in the discussion and it allows for an exchange of ideas in a non-stressful, non-judgmental, egalitarian forum. Dialogue brings down the barriers of apprehension and self-defense and allows people to share and build on thoughts in a most productive way. It often results in excellent planning and solutions, and people come away from the dialogue with a feeling of worth and well being.

Dialogue Focuses On:

listening	not just speaking
expressing	not fighting
being informed	not being right
win-win	not win-lose
hearing other points of view	not finding flaws
understanding	not winning
learning	not telling
informing	not impressing
all of us	not just me

Denial: Avoiding

Sometimes people pretend that a conflict does not exist or hope that it will just go away. When asked if there is something wrong, they say no. If asked why they are angry at a colleague, they say they are not angry. In all actuality there is something wrong and they are angry at that person. They are in denial about the conflict and are avoiding working on it. Sometimes this is a helpful method, sometimes it is not helpful. Teachers need to assess when it is not helpful and take steps to resolve it.

Aggression: Competing, Confronting

Sometimes people confront each other in lively and angry ways telling them what they want, not listening to the other person, and not caring what the other person feels or needs. They are aggressive and confrontational, competing to win this situation. They may be unable to communicate with the other person about the conflict for various reasons. They tried to ignore it but were pushed too far and exploded. Sometimes this is a helpful method, sometimes it is not helpful.

Control: Directing

Sometimes people direct others without listening. They do not want to spend a lot of time or energy on what appears to be a simple problem. They feel justified and informed on the topic and believe they have a sound solution. Sometimes this is a helpful method, sometimes it is not helpful. They may have experience in this routine kind of problem and their solution is welcome and most helpful, or they may lack understanding of key aspects of the problem and their solution is not helpful.

Sometimes people try solving things for someone else. It is most likely a sincere effort to help others, but it may not actually help. A more sound solution may come from the people who are in the problem themselves. They have the insight and the feelings to know what is workable when it is suggested.

Problem – Solving: Collaborating

Sometimes people talk it out, listening to discover the other's perspective, noting common ground and collaborating to create a solution that meets the needs of all. They engage in dialogue, name the issues in the problem and propose various solutions to resolve each issue. Sometimes this is a helpful method, sometimes it is not helpful.

Sources of Difficulty for the Inclusion Program

A Teacher Feels Intruded Upon

The principal announces in May that next year the school will begin an inclusion program. The classroom teacher is comfortable with her program and her teaching style and methods. She likes teaching third grade, and for the past four years has settled into a successful pattern. In September, a newcomer, a special education teacher who is mandated to work with her, steps into her classroom. She may feel put upon by a requirement that she did not ask for and had no say in. She also feels:

- Burdened by the thinking, planning, waiting and adjusting that comes with teamwork,

- Threatened by the presence of another teacher who may have a different style and philosophy, may disagree with her, may recommend changes or may criticize her teaching,

- Responsible to manage this other staff member, and

- Responsible for the results of the special education students' IEPs.

This special education teacher may be seen by the classroom teacher as an intruder. The classroom teacher is very comfortable and confident about her work as an autonomous educator. She has developed excellent methods over the past fifteen years that have always met with great success. She has ownership of her work. It is being taken away in a manner that is out of her control. The inclusion of special education students and their teacher into her classroom will disrupt a good thing. She may feel stolen from, disrupted, distrusted, unappreciated, dumped on, puzzled and undermined.

Personalities Do Not Match

There may be a difficult history in the working relationship of the two teachers who are assigned to the inclusion team. They have not gotten along well before and do not get along now.

The two teachers may not know each other. This can be beneficial since they can build their teamwork from scratch constructing a sound foundation, or it can be an encumbrance.

Teacher Bias

The classroom teacher may have a personal bias about special education students. She believes that special education students should not be in a regular classroom.

Veteran- Novice

The inclusion teaching team may consist of a veteran classroom teacher and a beginning special education teacher. The veteran may resent the principal for being put in a situation where she must follow the lead of a brand new teacher.

Leadership

Things can be destructive for the program if it is not supported by the principal or if the principal is ambiguous about her opinion on the topic.

Personnel changes

Often a program will succeed because all of the conditions were right when it began. But even a successful program may not maintain smooth operation and success when there are personnel changes.

Sources of Success for the Inclusion Program

Teachers Feel Grateful and Enthusiastic

The classroom teacher may feel grateful to have a partner to help her with the day to-day-education and management of twenty to thirty children. She may be relieved that she doesn't have to bear this burden alone, enthusiastic about the opportunities that the talents and wisdom of two professional educators can bring to creativity and successful teaching, or pleased to begin a new phase of her career.

Personalities Work Well With Understanding, Respect and Commitment

The inclusion team matches up very well. They both see the value of the program and appreciate the power and success that team teaching in the same room brings. They support each other with knowledge, talent, respect, handling student behavior, complementary styles and appreciation. Together they have the power of three.

Leadership

The opinion of school's leaders is an important factor in the success of the inclusion program. When leadership is supportive and sets a tone of commitment, inclusion has a greater chance for success. The principal must speak and act in a way that tells staff that inclusion is the philosophy of this school, the administration is committed to its success and she expects all staff to think and act likewise. It's not a temporary experiment, it's the way we do business.

Common Ground

The teachers who come together for the inclusion program have something in common. They are interested in and excited about the new work. They are being innovative risk takers who thrive on testing out cutting edge programs. They are veteran teachers who are ready and grateful for the change. They have worked together over the years and deeply respect each other.

Building a Good Working Relationship

Good teamwork requires communication and understanding: Understanding of the task at hand, knowing the talents and style of a teammate, turning the work over to a teammate at times, including each other in planning for elements, notifying each other of changes resolving issues as they arise. Things to keep in mind include:

1. Listening
2. Timing
3. Knowledge of the subject/task
4. Knowing roles
5. Naming roles
6. Stating expectations
7. Planning
8. Develop a usable conflict resolution plan
9. Commitment to the concept and philosophy of teamwork
10. Commitment to the concept and philosophy of inclusion
11. Being focused on the welfare of each child
12. Addressing conflict as it arises
13. Not letting issues fester
14. Talking to a trusted listener about concerns
15. Honoring each other's ideas and contributions
16. Communicating regularly to foster and maintain understanding

---

Communication and Respect

Communication between teachers on the inclusion team is the cornerstone of success. When people can communicate they can work together, plan, conduct lessons and solve problems. When people feel respected and show respect to each other, working relationships are usually productive. Listening and communicating create understanding and shows respect.

All teachers have a great deal to contribute to the team's performance. Establish communication from the start to foster creative dialogue, sharing of ideas, understanding, keeping each other informed, preventing confusion, solving problems and resolving conflict. If your team cannot communicate or resolve issues, enlist the help of a mediator to facilitate their discussion, advise them or otherwise help them resolve their issues.

Communication may be verbal or nonverbal. It may be knowledge of each other's movements and style that allows each teammate to know when to step in, when to stay back, when to step together, and when to hold each other back.

Listening

Listening is an essential skill in any relationship whether at work, at home, in a community, or in a place of worship. When people feel heard in a decision-making process or discussion, they are more accepting of the outcome. They are more invested in the plan, more willing to implement it, and more able to implement it effectively.

The key aspects of listening are hearing, acknowledging facts and feelings, and noting common ground.

Initial Communication

Team members come together with their own ideas, plans, expectations and assumptions. The only one who knows them is their owner. They must be communicated to the other team members as they come together. They must be committed to communication and understanding.

At the start of the life of the inclusion team, teachers must meet to discuss the following four concerns:

1. Purpose and Evaluation

The inclusion team and the administrators should meet to discuss the purpose and expectations of the program as well as the process and method of evaluation.

2. Goals

With the administrators, the team should identify the tangible and intangible goals for the program. Additionally, the team members should set their own goals together.

3. Expectations

The team members should meet to discuss their expectations of themselves, each other, and the administrators.

4. Roles and Responsibilities

The team needs to discuss and establish the roles of each member. What we each do, what we do together, what we do not need to do, what we should leave for the other to do.

A Partnering Session

To foster good communication, clarify expectations, solve some initial problems and plan for future problem-solving and conflict resolution, the team members and perhaps the administrators should meet for a partnering session to lay out their plans, with the following agenda:

- Explain the purpose of the program.

- Identify the characteristics of a good partner and partnership values.

- Brainstorm a list of words and phrases that characterize a good partner, i.e., good listener, trustworthy, reliable, competent, etc.

- Finalize the list and post it near the teacher desk or by the door to remind the team members of their own expectations.

Partnership values include:

1. Open and honest communications

2. Respect and trust

3. Fair dealing

4. Concern for the interest of others

5. Helping each other achieve goals

6. Taking responsibility for our own actions

7. Keeping an open mind concerning the actions of others. Do not judge. Assume the best.

In addition:

- Identify the strengths of each member. Brainstorm together the talents, knowledge, experience and other strengths of each member. A basic part of good teamwork is recognizing the talents and strengths of the teammate. It's also important for teammates to name their own weaknesses and areas to improve. Knowing what I do well is important for me to know and for my colleagues to know. Knowing what I do not do well is important for me to know and for my colleagues to know.

- Name the common ground they share. What commonalities do the team members already have: interests, talents, feelings, etc.

- Name the problems they anticipate with the program. Make a list of the challenges, difficulties, problems and conflicts that already face the team and a list of problems that they anticipate along the way.

- Develop solutions to those problems now. Taking one problem at a time, brainstorm options and possible solutions to those problems.

- Make a plan. Develop methods for dealing with those problems and new ones when they arise. How, when and where will the team identify problems and resolve them? At a regular team meeting take time for naming problems. These problems may be tangible such as needed books, or they may be intangible such as feeling unjustly blamed for how science class went on Tuesday.

Ongoing Communication

The team must establish a routine system for communicating and resolving issues. Ask and resolve:

- What methods will we establish for ongoing communication? i.e., daily, semi-weekly, weekly planning sessions.

- What method will we establish for identifying and resolving issues that arise?

Conflict Resolution/Problem — Solving Plan, Skills, Method

Problems and conflicts will arise as the program goes on. There may be problems that involve student-student, teacher-student issues, as well as teacher-parent, parent-student, teacher-administrator and teacher-teacher issues. It may be helpful to set aside time during each team meeting to identify the latest issues. Early detection and naming of problems prevent conflict and gets things solved early. When it is decided that there are problems involving different people, follow these steps:

- Get the people together who need to be talking.

- Set up some communication ground rules at the beginning of the meeting: i.e., taking turns, be respectful.
- Give everyone opportunities to speak.
- Name the common ground among the participants.
- Name the issues and problems to be solved.
- Brainstorm solutions together.
- Find agreement.
- Write up a plan.

A Dialogue Process for Problem Solving and Decision Making

The following is a step by step process for having a productive dialogue to create understanding and resolve issues that arise.

- Listen to each other. Having time for each to speak (taking turns, letting each person finish). Acknowledging the other's thoughts (occasionally summarizing facts & feelings). Asking questions to understand.
- Name common ground between each other
- Name differences between each other
- Identify and name issues or problems to solve
- Brainstorm ideas, options, and possible solutions
- Find agreement for these ideas
- Make a plan from these agreements

In this dialogue, go easy on the people and work hard on the problems.

In this dialogue, go easy on the people and work hard on the problems. When having a dialogue about issues and plans, keep the focus on the problems at hand without blaming a specific person. There is a common pattern of saying that he or she is the problem. Instead, identify the behavior or outside influence that is the problem such as: Being late, or lack of funding. And keep names out of it as much as possible. If we name the issue at hand, you can work on resolving it together, collaboratively as a team.

Enlist an Intermediary

If the team can't communicate or resolve issues they should enlist the help of an intermediary to facilitate their discussion, advise them or otherwise help them resolve their issues. If the team members remain in conflict over unresolved issues, their ability to serve the students will be impaired.

We Can Talk About It

Here is another approach to one-to-one or group dialogue/problem-solving.

We Can Talk About It

A simple version of the mediation process
and the negotiation process.

Thanks for coming.
Show respect.

Can we take turns?
Set ground rules.

What happened?
*Listen to each other point of view. Listen for and
acknowledge (summarize) facts & feelings.*

What would you like to solve?
Identify issues to be resolved. (Don't just blame people.)

How would you like to solve it?
Generate options. Brainstorm solutions.

What would you agree to?
Note common ground. Find agreement.

Thanks for coming.
Express gratitude.

*Note: Sit or stand so that everyone can see each other.
Choose a good time for this discussion.
Allow enough time for this discussion.
Use a non-judgmental, non-punitive manner.
Remember: This is a collaboration, not a competition.*

Bibliography

Affleck, J., Lowenbraun, S., Madge, S. (1990). Social Effects of Integrated Classroom and resource room/regular class placement on elementary students with learning disabilities.

Journal of Learning Disabilities, 23, 439-445.

Buswell, Barbara E., Schaffner, Beth C. (1991). Opening Doors.

Colorado Springs, CO.: Peak Parents Center, Inc.

Kukic, Steven (1994). Rhetoric to Action: Inclusion at Work in the State of Utah.

Counterpoint p.6. Horsham, PA

National Association of State Board of Education (NASBE). Study Group (1992).

Winners All: A Call for Inclusive Schools. Alexandria, VA:

I. Stainback, S. Stainback, W. Thousand, J. Villa R. (1992).

Restructuring for caring and effective education: An Administrative Guide to Creating Heterogeneous Schools.

  Richard Schattman (EDS.), The Franklin Northwest, Supervisory Union

  A Case Study of an Inclusive School System. (Chapter 7).

  Baltimore, Maryland. Pauls H. Brooks Publishing Company.

Vargo, Joe and Vargo, Ro (1993) Parents: A 'typical' classroom is the only choice.

  Counterpoint p.5. Horsham, PA

Wiles, J. (1999). Curriculum Essentials: A Resource for Educators.

  Boston: Allyn & Bacon. ISBN: 0-20527-988-0.